THE PRECIOUS BLOOD

THE PRECIOUS BLOOD

An enlightened study on the different aspects of Christ's blood as revealed in the Scriptures.

by David Alsobrook

"Now the God of peace, that brought again from the dead our Lord Jesus, that Great Shepherd of the sheep, through the blood of the everlasting covenant, *make you perfect in every good work to do His will . . . " (Hebrews 13:20-21a).*

LOVINGLY DEDICATED

to my wife, Dianne,

who has helped her husband

obey God

Cover design: Em Lachance

This book has been printed in India in the Telugu language by the Christian Free Tract Center.

First printing September 1977
Second printing February 1978
Third printing December 1978
Fourth printing June 1979
Fifth printing December 1980

Library of Congress Catalog Card Number: 77-072843
International Standard Book Number: 0-89221-034-6

CONTENTS

PREFACE

Every serious Christian has studied with sincere desire to understand the teachings of God's Word. A basic topic all encounter is the blood truth that runs from Genesis to Revelation. We have attempted in this book to show why the blood is so very important and necessary in the total plan for man's redemption. All who hunger for God will find rich nuggets of blood truths and will better realize the provisions Jesus Christ has supplied for each and all.

It will be necessary to keep your Bible alongside as you read this volume. A thorough reading and understanding of the truths brought forth in each chapter will enrich your spiritual life and deepen your appreciation of Christ for all He has done in our behalf.

May the Lord bless this book in the reading as He did in the writing. Please read the contents with an open mind and heart. There may be some things brought forth that you have not heard before. There is much more in the blood of Christ than just the forgiveness of sins.   —David Alsobrook

Chapter One

THE BLOOD COVERING

The Scripture hints that prior to the Fall in the Garden of Eden both Adam and Eve were clothed with the divine presence in such a form as the Shekinah glory, so that while they were naked in the sense that no material cloth was on their bodies they were covered with a spiritual presence that hid their nakedness from their eyes. "And they were both naked, the man and his wife, and were not ashamed" (Gen. 2:25). When they partook of the forbidden fruit sin entered the world and the conscious presence of God immediately departed. "And the eyes of them both were opened (uncovered from the presence of God), and they knew (or could see) that they were naked . . . " (Gen. 3:7).

Notice that Adam and Eve were used to a covering. Due to the habitual fellowship pattern that God had previously established with our first parents they knew that "in the cool of the day" He would come walking in the garden that He might fellowship with them and they with Him. Up to that day the glory of His presence abode upon their countenances and

9

they would behold Him. Now uncovered, they were ashamed to be in His presence so they "sewed fig leaves together, and made themselves aprons" (Gen. 3:7). They knew from past experience they could only approach God covered.* Those aprons were man's first attempt to make himself acceptable to God by his own efforts. The fig leaves just did not compare with the previous glory. "All our righteousnesses are as filthy rags" (Isa. 64:6). They knew God would not be fooled by their manufactured coverings. So when the Lord came walking to them they hid themselves from His presence (glory) among the trees.

Hide and Seek

Whenever the glory and conscious presence of God flows in meetings, and people leave feeling uncomfortable in God's presence it is due to the fact they are not right with God, and there is something in their lives they are trying to hide. If something in you hides from light it is surely darkness.

Notice God's question, "And the LORD God called unto Adam, and said unto him, *Where art thou?*" God's voice echoed through the garden, "Adam, where are you?" When man hides, God seeks. Adam knew he was caught, "And he said, I heard thy voice in the garden, and I WAS AFRAID, BECAUSE I WAS NAKED; and I hid myself."

---

* God has never condoned nakedness. The Gadarene demoniac wore no clothes prior to his deliverance. As soon as the Master delivered him, however, he was quick to dress himself. Sitting at Jesus' feet the city dwellers found him "clothed and in his right mind" (see Luke 8:27, 35). Eternally the saints will be "clothed with white robes" (Rev. 7:9).

Adam was afraid because he was naked, he was naked because he had sinned. Before the holiness of God he was openly exposed with no covering. Fear entered the world with sin.

Substitution Death

Adam knew death was his punishment. When God took man and put him in the garden He had warned him, "Of every tree of the garden thou mayest freely eat: But of the tree of the knowledge of good and evil, thou shalt not eat of it: for *in the day* thou eatest thereof thou shalt surely die" (Gen. 2:16-17). Up to this dark day Adam had never seen death, for death came by sin. Never had he observed death in any fashion. He only knew by revelation what death could mean. Spiritually he and Eve died as soon as they ate of the tree of knowledge. Now they stood before God a short time later awaiting physical death. Instead, God placed a curse upon man and departed. A short time later He brought to our human parents coats of skins still warm and wet with blood. Adam and Eve had never seen blood before. Innocent animals had been put to death by God. Mysteriously, somehow, the Lord removed the animal bodies and provided a covering for man. When Adam and Eve were clothed with these coats they were reckoned dead in the animals. Let's examine very closely this short verse of Scripture containing profound truth. "Unto Adam also and to his wife did the LORD God make coats of skins, and clothed them" (Gen. 3:21).

There is a rule of interpretation in Bible study known as *the law of the first mention.* This principle teaches that whenever a topic first appears in Scripture there are certain basic truths laid down that are never revoked and govern throughout the whole of the Bible. Although the word "blood" is not used we know this is what the verse is all about. There are six apparent laws or principles laid out in this one short sentence.

God Requires Shedding Of Blood For Sin

The Lord made coats of skins from animal(s). In so doing its blood was shed and poured out on the ground. Shedding of blood was necessary to provide remission of transgression. " . . . without shedding of blood is no remission (forgiveness)" (Heb. 9:22).

Sinner Must Be Covered By The Blood

Not only was the substitute slain but its blood was applied to Adam and to his wife when God clothed them with its skins. It is not enough that blood is shed; it must also be accepted. Each individual must receive God's provision for himself. Jesus' blood has been shed for the whole world (see 1 John 2:1-2) but His sacrifice must be accepted by a person before the blood atones (covers) for his sin. No one will go to hell because his sin has not been taken care of, but because he refused to accept the atonement. After the blood has been shed it must be applied. This covering of blood is stated forthright in Leviticus 17:11: "For the life of the flesh is in the blood: and I have given it to you upon the altar to make an atonement for your souls: for it is the blood that maketh an atonement for the soul." Atonement is the Hebrew word *Kaphar* which means to cover and make reconciliation. "It is the blood that makes an atonement" would mean then that only the blood makes a covering (which God accepts). Bloodless coverings are unacceptable to God. *It is the blood that makes a covering for the sinner.*

A person's natural life is maintained by the blood that flows in his veins. Hence, "For the life of the flesh (natural life) is in the blood . . . " When blood pours unstopped from a person's body he will soon die. Each deserves that his blood be poured out due to sin, but the perfect God/Man (Jesus Christ) so lived that He never sinned (see Hebrews 4:15) and was not worthy of death (see Luke 23:22). Yet when Jesus laid down His life for the sheep—for no man took it from Him—He did so by pouring out His blood for "the life . . . is in the blood" (see John 10:11, 18). He laid down His life for the sheep; gave His blood for us or to us. He no longer has any of His blood in His glorified body. We have it! When His crucified body was resurrected it became glorified *flesh* and *bone* (but no blood). While it is true that *"flesh* and *blood* cannot inherit the kingdom of God," (1 Cor. 15:50) flesh and bone can for Jesus said *following* His resurrection to a room of terrified disciples, "Behold my hands and my feet, that it is I myself: handle me, and see; for *a spirit hath not flesh and bones, as ye see me have"* (Luke 24:39). When Thomas put his finger in the print of the nails and thrust his hands into Christ's side there is no mention that Thomas had blood on his hands for there was none.*

---

*Notice also in John 20:25, 27 that the glorified Christ does not have nail-scarred hands, as though they healed, but nail-pierced hands. Jesus instructed Thomas to thrust his hand into His side. His wounds are forever there. Forever Jesus will bear in His body the marks of our redemption and we shall gaze upon Him even as Thomas and the other disciples did (See also Zechariah 13:6).

The *believer* is covered with the blood of Christ. Our body's life is maintained by our natural blood. Our spirit's life is maintained by Christ's blood. "The life is in the blood." Jesus' blood was sprinkled upon the mercy seat in heaven almost two milleniums ago and is still efficacious for the believer.

God Provided The Sacrifice

Here in this first example of blood sacrifice the transgressors did not provide their own lamb but God made the provision and did not require Adam and Eve to bring a sacrifice animal. Why did God do this in the garden when later throughout the Old Testament (with one exception) each man had to bring his own sacrifice?

The answer can be seen in the fact that thousands of years later God provided the perfect sacrifice referred to as "the lamb of God" and that through His lamb was provided the "robe of righteousness and garment of salvation" for each of us. The coats of skins He provided for the first man and woman are types of the salvation provided us in Jesus Christ.

The one other place in all the Old Testament where God provided the sacrifice and did not require the sacrificer to bring it to the place of sacrifice is in Genesis the twenty-second chapter. Without going into all the detail of Abraham's journey to Moriah to offer Isaac upon the altar let us quickly notice some key points. Please read Genesis 22:1-14 and follow along in your Bible as you study these points. Our comments will help the reader understand the substitution principle.

V. 2—God really would not have accepted Isaac as a sacrifice since an age-old requirement is that the sacrifice be without sin, pictured in animal sacrifices as "without spot and blemish." Isaac was a sinner. God was testing Abraham's faith and obedience (v. 1).

V. 4—During the three days of travel to the place of sacrifice Abraham came to a place of faith in God that even if Isaac, the child of promise, was slain God would raise him from the dead.

> "By faith Abraham, when he was tried, offered up Isaac; and he that had received the promises offered up his only begotten son, of whom it was said, That in Isaac shall thy seed be called: accounting that God was able *to raise him up, even from the dead;* from whence also he received him in a figure" (Heb. 11:17-19).

V. 5—Abraham tells his young men to wait while he and Isaac go to the place of worship and demonstrates his faith that Isaac will be raised when he infers both will return again to the waiting men.

V. 7—Shows that children knew much about blood sacrifice as Isaac listed the items used such as the fire and the wood but asks his father about the lamb needed to offer a burnt offering. The parents trained their children about blood sacrifice by example and instruction and passed information down to the generations in this manner until the law was given.

V. 8—A statement which reveals the nature of Jesus' sacrifice: *"God will provide himself a lamb."* Abraham did not end up actually slaying Isaac, his only begotten son through Sarah, but God did actually lay upon His Son the iniquity of us all.

V. 10—The ultimate test of Abraham's obedience.

15

The knife would have gone into Isaac's chest had not the angel of the Lord called unto Abraham from heaven.

V. 13—A ram caught in a thicket was the first fulfillment of the promise, "God will provide Himself a lamb." Jesus, the Lamb of God (from the Father's bosom) ultimately, perfectly, and absolutely fulfilled the promise. Ram (mature lamb) was offered IN THE STEAD of Isaac. Substitution principle once again enacted and revealed.

V. 14—Abraham's revelation of Jehovah's redemption is explained in one of the seven redemptive names of God given in the Old Testament. "JEHOVAH-JIREH" which means *the Lord will see (to it)*; or, as it is commonly taken to mean, *God supplies.*

God Covers The Sinner With The Blood

Notice in our text (Genesis 3:21) the phrase "and clothed them" which could also be read "and (He) clothed them." God not only provided the sacrifice and made the coverings of skins, but also clothed Adam and Eve with them. They did not clothe themselves. When it comes to the robe of righteousness and the garment of salvation we do not put it on, God puts it on us. He clothes us with righteousness.

"I will greatly rejoice in the LORD, my soul shall be joyful in my God; for *He hath clothed me* with the garments of salvation, *He hath covered me* with the robe of righteousness . . . " (Isa. 61:10).

Paul expressed it in this manner, "It is God that justifieth" (Rom. 8:33). We cannot do it ourselves, as sinners we repent and believe, but God regenerates us on the basis of the blood of Christ.

16

Innocent Dies For The Guilty

The animal(s) the Lord slew in the stead of Adam and Eve had never done wrong or committed evil. They were innocent and yet they died. If this seems unfair think how "much more" unfair it seems that "Christ died for the ungodly" (Rom. 5:6). He was more than innocent, He was perfectly righteous. Righteousness is innocence proven. He was "in all points tempted" and "yet without sin" (Heb. 4:15). The prince of the world (Satan) had not one legal claim on Him (John 14:30). Throughout the Old Testament the guilt of the transgressor is passed from himself to his sacrifice, and the innocence (or righteousness as with Jesus) is transferred by imputation to the transgressor.

Jesus foretold His offering of Himself in our place. "Even as the Son of man came not to be ministered unto, but to minister, and to give his life a ransom for many" (Matt. 20:28). He gave Himself a ransom for, or instead of many.

God Brought Judgment Upon The Sacrifice

In the first example we see the Lord evidently slew the sacrifice Himself. Throughout the rest of the Old Testament the sinner or the priest did the slaying. The first mention principle points us once again to the New Testament where Jesus experiences judgment in our behalf. Eight hundred years before Christ Isaiah sees the crucifixion in progress and prophetically states in past tense, " . . . the LORD hath laid on him the iniquity of us all . . . Yet it pleased the LORD to bruise him; he hath put him to grief: when Thou shalt make his soul an offering for sin . . . " (Isa. 53:6, 10).

Paul, through the revelation given him acknowledges, "For he hath made him (the Father has made the Son) to be (to be can be omitted) sin for us, who knew no sin; that we might be made the righteousness of God in Him" (2 Cor. 5:21). Jesus bore our sins in His *body* (1 Peter 2:24) and abolished the enmity in His *flesh* (Ephesians 2:15). Jesus experienced the wrath of God for us (see Habakkuk 1:13; Matthew 27:46) only upon the cross—at death His suffering was complete—and now we experience "peace with God" through our Lord Jesus Christ (Rom. 5:1).

Adam and Eve's dealings with blood sacrifices were not finished in the Garden of Eden. They evidently offered blood sacrifices after they were driven out, and down through the years taught their children to offer sacrifice when they became sin conscious, as we shall see in the next chapter.

Chapter Two

WHY GOD ACCEPTED ABEL AND REJECTED CAIN

The blood theology has been rejected by many people in our time. Such intellectually-guided ministers label this message "the butcher shop gospel" and mock those who claim their sins have been "washed in the blood of the Lamb."

Greatly renown seminaries train young preachers that the blood message is "socially unattractive and unsuitable" for the thinking class of America. "Why would an all-wise God desire to see blood?" The same serpent who influenced Cain speaks to people the same way today with the same ideas.

My heart sank when a reportedly good minister stated, "The blood of Jesus is not important, just His death was, if He had been strangled to death it would have sufficed." We were quick to point out that the ancient Israelites were forbidden to offer that which was strangled as were the early Christians forbidden to partake of strangled meats. We could not accept Christ as our sacrifice nor could we partake of Him had He been strangled. This one example shows how Satan is seeking to take away from the importance of

Christ's blood today. He de-emphasizes its importance then destroys the blood concept in the thinking of even conservative/evangelical churches. Many have removed the songs about the blood from their hymnals. In the liberal translations *haima* is rendered "death" rather than "blood" again and again.

We now go to the Bible for the first example of such demonized thinking. We do not have to go far from the first blood covering in the third chapter of Genesis. In Genesis chapter four we see man's first attempt to approach God and find His favor the bloodless way. This man's attempt to find acceptance by God and access to Him without blood ended in failure. How pitiably sad it is today that those who follow Cain's *pattern* will end with Cain's *punishment* —isolation from God. Let's turn our attention to the Scriptures for a verse study of Genesis 4:1-7.

Conceived Once—Bore Twice

"And Adam *knew* Eve his wife; and she *conceived*, and *bare* Cain, and said, I have gotten a man from the Lord. (Perhaps Eve thought her first-born son would be the seed that would bruise the serpent's head [cf. Gen. 3:15]). And again she *bare* his brother Abel."

Notice the words "knew" and "conceived" appear once while the word "bare" (bore) appears twice. Throughout the Bible it is the usual procedure to record each conception with each birth. When a mother has given birth to two infants and conceived only once her children are twins. " . . . she bare Cain . . . and again she bare his brother Abel." She bare and again she bare. It would seem to the serious student of the Scriptures that there exists a strong possibility Cain and Abel were twin brothers. Have you ever noticed the age difference implied in the family Bible pictures of Cain and Abel? Cain is full grown and bearded, while Abel is smooth-faced and much smaller. There is no substantiation for this in all the Word of God.

The truth is these boys were men before they ever brought an offering to the Lord. "And Abel was a keeper of sheep (shepherd), but Cain was a tiller of the ground (farmer). And *in process of time* it came to pass . . . " Abel and Cain were both occupied in a livelihood, grown up, and fully responsible. They were not irresponsible youths. A surface reading coupled with tradition often leads to a misconception about their age. The Bible skips maybe 20 or more years between the first and second sentence in verse two. Cain and Abel did not sacrifice until they were on their own. As children they were covered by their parents' offerings of blood. " . . . else were your children unclean; but now are they holy" (1 Cor. 7:14). Even as early in the Scriptures as Genesis 4 we see the Bible teaches the age of accountability. Later, as young adults, each had to bring his own sacrifice. Cain had to bring his for himself and Abel likewise (cf. Phil. 2:12). The phrase "in process of time" further shows the time lapse involved.

Hearing God's Word

Adam and Eve had learned from the coverings God had clothed them with in the garden to use the shed blood of an animal substitute whenever their conscience convicted them of sin. They passed this on to their sons by example and instruction. As they laid the lamb upon the rock they would say, "Children,

21

this is the way to remove the punishment of your evildoings." In later life Cain well knew he was rejecting God's method of approach when he offered fruit. These boys had grown into men watching their parents offer unto God animal sacrifices of blood. They had heard their words of instruction concerning blood. One or two Scriptures bring out this point:

"By faith Abel offered unto God a more excellent sacrifice than Cain, by which he obtained witness that he was righteous" (Heb. 11:4).

"So then faith cometh by hearing, and hearing by the word of God" (Rom. 10:17).

If Abel offered his sacrifice to God by faith, where did he get it? How does faith come? "BY HEARING!" Hearing what? "THE WORD OF GOD!" But how did Abel hear the Word of God?

Before we answer this question let's notice that Eve told the serpent what "God hath said" in Genesis 3:2-3 (although she misquoted it some) and yet when God said (in chapter 2:16-17) the very words she referred to, she was not yet created! Notice, "And the LORD God commanded *the man*, saying, Of every tree of the garden thou mayest freely eat: But of the tree of the knowledge of good and evil, thou shalt not eat of it: for in the day thou eatest thereof thou shalt surely die." Only Adam was present when God spoke these words. Eve was not created until later (verse 22). This would answer the question, "How did Abel (as well as Cain) hear God's Word when they had no Bible, etc.?" From their father, Adam, of course. Just as Adam had previously taught the woman God's commandment he (and perhaps Eve also) trained their children in the way they should go according to the instructions God had given them in the garden. This is a biblical concept.

Offering The Curse

Modern scholars erroneously teach that both Abel and Cain were ignorant of how to approach God. They insist that Abel offered a lamb only because he was a shepherd and Cain offered fruit because he was a farmer. Such was not the case. Cain knew he was rejecting God's only method of approach. Cain disbelieved the word of God he had been taught by his parents. Cain's bloodless sacrifice was not due to ignorance; it was a willful rejection of the divine revelation. No doubt his parents had told all their children (evidently Cain and Abel had unmentioned sisters) the full story of their sin in the garden and the resultant curse God had placed on the serpent, the woman, the man, and *the ground.* "Cursed is the ground for thy sake . . . thorns also and thistles shall it bring forth . . . " (Gen. 3:17-18). This fact clearly reveals the rebellious attitude Cain held toward God for he offered what God had cursed, in an attempt to receive blessing! He would have been better to not have offered anything than to bring the curse as an offering. He openly flaunted God's method and mocked His Word. The wonder is not that God sent no fire upon Cain's sacrifice. The marvel is that God sent no fire upon Cain! Even in this early period of time we see God's matchless mercy. He even offered Cain a second chance. "If thou doest well (come God's way), shalt thou not be accepted?" God beseeched Cain following his offering of grain (see v. 7). Cain still had opportunity to

23

repent of his rebellion and offer to God the sacrifice of righteousness. God would have respected (accepted) an offering of blood from Cain as readily as He did from Abel "for there is no respect of persons with God" (Rom. 2:11).

The Fire Falls

It is difficult to write this in a completely orderly fashion since the exposition demands we get ahead of the order of events in an endeavor to bring forth each truth. Going back to Genesis 4 let's take up with verse 3: "And in process of time it came to pass, that Cain brought of the fruit of the ground an offering unto the LORD. And Abel, he also brought of the firstlings of his flock and of the fat thereof. And the LORD had respect unto Abel and to his offering: But unto Cain and his offering he had not respect . . . " (vs. 3-5).

The question posed by these verses is, "In what way did God respect an offering, and how was it that both sacrificers knew which sacrifice God accepted and which offering He refused?" In answering this question we point out that very obviously there was an OPEN DEMONSTRATION that was clearly SUPERNATURAL from God. This witness, or testimony of acceptance, (see Hebrews 11:4) was openly manifest or VISIBLE to human sight. There was no possibility of mistaking which offering God respected.

In no less than a dozen places the Old Testament states that God showed His acceptance of an offered sacrifice by sending fire from heaven consuming it. Here are only a few examples:

"And there came a fire out from before
the LORD, and consumed upon the altar

the burnt offering and the fat: which when all the people saw, they shouted, and fell on their faces" (Lev. 9:24).

"Then the fire of the LORD fell, and consumed the burnt sacrifice . . . " (1 Kings 18:38).

"Now when Solomon had made an end of praying, the fire came down from heaven, and consumed the burnt offering and the sacrifices; and the glory of the LORD filled the house" (2 Chron. 7:1).

It is our studied conviction that, " . . . God testifying of his (Abel's) gifts . . . " (Heb. 11:4) refers to *a fire witness* that involuntarily from human effort descended rapidly out of the sky upon the slain firstling of Abel's flock. This fire typifies one aspect of the Holy Spirit who falls in answer to the blood of Christ. Upon Cain's beautiful bouquet of luscious fruit there was not even so much as a spark from above. A work of the flesh will never bring the blessing a sacrifice in the Spirit brings.

Another important observation from the particular passage points to the truth that a person is either accepted or rejected on the basis of his sacrifice. It was because God accepted Abel's sacrifice that He accepted Abel. Likewise, Cain was rejected because his sacrifice was rejected. Do not be misled into thinking Abel was automatically righteous prior to the sacrifice. " . . . he obtained witness that he was righteous," because he came offering God's way. Had he been sinless he would have needed no sacrifice. Abel was just as much a sinner as Cain. Abel was a man. The Word declares, "All (men) have sinned, and come short of the glory of God" (Rom. 3:23). One is accepted by God today only because the Sacrifice Himself is accepted.

Bloodless Religions Are Evil

Cain hated the blood because he was of the devil. "Not as Cain, who was of that wicked one, and slew his brother. And wherefore slew he him? Because his own works were evil, and his brother's righteous" (1 John 3:12). The Apostle John tells us whose influence Cain was under when he offered his fruit. Cain's bloodless sacrifice was due to satanic deception. When his offering was refused (God does not condone Satan's methods) and his brother's accepted, jealousy to the point of rage came over Cain. "And Cain was very wroth, and his countenance fell" (Gen. 4:5). A spirit of anger entered into Cain's emotions and a few days later a spirit of murder came in. Hatred always opens the door to murder if left unchecked. "Whosoever hateth his brother is a murderer," (1 John 3:15) the Apostle informs us only three verses after mentioning Cain's evil works. Cain's hatred of Abel led to a premeditated plot to destroy his brother (cf. John 10:10). God saw it in Cain and tried to bring him to repentance. "And the LORD said unto Cain, Why art thou wroth? and why is thy countenance fallen? If thou doest well, shalt thou not be accepted? and if thou doest not well, sin lieth at the door. And unto thee shall be his desire, and thou shalt rule over him" (Gen. 4:6-7).

The Cain Spirit

It is hinted that Cain's attack upon Abel occurred

sometime after the offering of sacrifice. "And Cain talked with Abel his brother: and *it came to pass*, when they were in the field, that Cain rose up against Abel his brother, and slew him" (v. 8). Isn't it interesting that the first anger and murder occurred on the basis of religion? In the body of Christ today *the Cain spirit* is moving forth in ever-widening circles. Brother rises up against brother and through words kills the reputation of one Jesus loves. Malicious gossip, slander, backbiting are a few of the tools this spirit uses to accomplish its destructive task. Are you envious when another is moved to a higher position? Do you attack another's character without justifiable grounds?

Perhaps Satan moved into Cain's thought life weeks before this time when he realized that were he to offer a blood sacrifice he would have to obtain the lamb from his brother's flock. Or, maybe, as a boy watching the bleeding sacrifices die as his parents offered sacrifice to God a seducing spirit would reason with his carnal mind saying, "How unattractive!" When it came his time to go before God something whispered to him, "This beautiful bouquet would please God more." How true it is that blood sacrifice *is* ugly! It is not a beautiful picture at all. "The wages of sin is death," and was never meant to occur in God's beautiful creation. If the devil ever tempts you to reject the blood of the cross on the idea that it is ugly remind yourself . . . SO IS SIN. Man's refusal to the blood all through the ages is due to his refusal to acknowledge his sinfulness. Without blood sacrifice, however, there is no remission of sin (see Hebrews 9:22).

A Fugitive And A Vagabond

Banishment from society and isolation from the deity was the punishment God placed on Cain. How true, yet sad, it is that all who reject God's provision in Jesus Christ are already banished from fellowship with the saints, and unless they repent will ultimately be isolated from God. In Genesis 4 verse 9 we see a type of the conscience, "And the LORD said unto Cain, Where is Abel thy brother? And he said, I know not: Am I my brother's keeper?" Cain lied to God. "And he said, What hast thou done? the voice of thy brother's blood crieth unto me from the ground" (v. 10). Science has proven that shed blood cries from the ground. A machine has been developed which records the sound of dying blood. Abel's blood cried unto the Lord from the ground. Jesus' blood cried unto the Father from the foot of the cross. The writer of Hebrews gives a parallel distinction between the cry of Jesus' blood and that of Abel's.

"And to Jesus the mediator of the new
covenant, and to the blood of sprinkling,
that SPEAKETH BETTER THINGS than
that of Abel" (Heb. 12:24).

The New International Version says, "speaks a better word." The better things or better word Christ's blood speaks is a word of *mercy*, whereas Abel's blood cried out for *vengeance*. Judgment fell on Cain for the blood of his brother, but justification comes to us today when we accept the blood of the Lamb of God. Due to our transgressions Jesus was smitten. His blood is sprinkled upon the mercy seat in heaven at this hour. Whenever we approach God and claim Jesus' work as our basis of access "we have boldness to enter into the holiest" (Heb. 10:19).

The judgment which fell upon the first murderer was a rejection of his future toil upon the earth, and banishment as a wanderer upon the earth. "And now art thou cursed from the earth, which hath opened her mouth to receive thy brother's blood from thy hand; when thou tillest the ground, it shall not henceforth yield unto thee her strength; a fugitive and a vagabond shalt thou be in the earth. And Cain said unto the LORD, *My punishment is greater than I can bear*" (Gen. 4:11-13).

Chapter Three

LAMB REQUIREMENTS

Our precious Saviour is referred to as A LAMB some 33 times in the New Testament. It is amazing for at that same age He became the perfect lamb sacrifice for the world. Old Testament sacrifice laws and prophecies concerning the Messiah point to Him as a lamb almost countless times. The Law laid down certain basic requirements concerning blood sacrifice. Moses' use of the lamb for sacrifice offerings pictures the nature and character of Christ.

The Lamb Must Be Perfect

The Passover Lamb which marked the beginning of the exodus of Israel from Egypt could not have a blemish on its coat. "Your lamb shall be without blemish, a male of the first year . . . " (Exod. 12:5). Later in Leviticus 22:20 a law of sacrifices read, "But whatsoever hath a blemish that shall ye not offer: for it shall not be acceptable for you." In His instructions about the feast of the firstfruits the Lord says through Moses, "And ye shall offer that day when ye wave the sheaf an he lamb without blemish of the first year for a burnt offering unto the LORD" (Lev. 23:12). This offering typifies the resurrection of our Lord. "But now is Christ risen from the dead, and become the firstfruits of them that slept. . . . But every man in his own order: Christ the firstfruits; afterward they that are Christ's at his coming" (1 Cor. 15:20, 23).

Jesus fulfilled these requirements given in the law. He was a male, a man of the first year, in the prime of life and perfect spirit, soul, and body. Peter tells us we are not redeemed with corruptible things, "But with the precious blood of Christ, as of a lamb without blemish and without spot" (1 Pet. 1:19).

Jesus was without blemish physically. He was a perfect man. Because He never sinned He was not worthy of death and its forerunner, sickness. His acquaintance with sickness and pain all took place within the last few hours of His natural life. During the 33 years He walked among men He was the perfect specimen of health. The body of the last Adam was just as sovereignly created by God in the womb of Mary as was the body of the first Adam formed by God from the clay. There was no sin in His flesh until He laid it down at the cross, neither any sickness until the whipping post. The first Adam had a natural body prior to the Fall that was sinless and sickless until he disobeyed God. Sickness entered into the first Adam's flesh only after sin.

Jesus was "without spot" spiritually. He "was in all points tempted like as we are, yet without sin" (Heb. 4:15). He "knew no sin" by transgression (2 Cor. 5:21). He was "holy, harmless, (and) undefiled" (Heb. 7:26). Satan tried every trick on Jesus that he ever tries on anyone. Today we have no

31

excuse if we do not overcome as Jesus overcame for He has provided all the necessary equipment. Jesus was the perfect lamb.

Lamb Was To Be A Sin Offering

Throughout the Word we see the lamb offered instead of the sinner. Abel's lamb atoned for Abel's sin. Isaac's lamb atoned for Isaac. The Law made provision for bringing "a lamb for a sin offering" (Lev. 4:32). The Lamb of God is "the propitiation for our sins" (1 John 2:2).

Lamb Was To Be Slain

The law of cleansing lepers specifically instructed, "And the priest shall take one he lamb, and offer him for a trespass offering . . . And he shall slay the lamb . . . " (Lev. 14:12-13). Isaiah prophesied concerning Christ saying, " . . . He was cut off out of the land of the living . . . " (Isa. 53:8). John heard "the voice of many angels . . . saying with loud voice, Worthy is *the Lamb that was slain* to receive power, and riches, and wisdom, and strength, and honour, and glory, and blessing" (Rev. 5:11-12).

A Lamb For The World

In the Old Testament we see *a lamb for a man* in many examples: Genesis 4:4; 22:13; Leviticus 14:11-14 and many others. The passover pictures *a lamb for a house* (family). "Speak ye unto all the congregation of Israel, saying, In the tenth day of this month they shall take to them every man a lamb, . . for an house" (Exod. 12:3). The Day of Atonement demonstrated the offering of *a lamb for a nation:* see Leviticus 16:29-34; 23:26-32; Hebrews 9:7, 25.

Each of these point to Jesus.

It is not until the New Testament, however, that we see *a lamb for the world.* "The next day John seeth Jesus coming unto him, and saith, Behold *the Lamb of God,* which taketh away *the sin of the world"* (John 1:29). Do you see the circle ever widening? It begins with a lamb for a man, spreads to a lamb for a house, increases to a lamb for a nation (Israel), and ultimately finishes in A LAMB FOR THE WORLD. Jesus is the ultimate Lamb. His sacrifice is greater than that of calves and sheep. So perfectly perfect and completely complete is His offering of Himself that He could say of His work, "It is finished" (John 19:30). No further need for any more blood sacrifices. His sacrifice accomplished the will of the Father in removing sin from the very conscience of the worshipper (see Hebrews 9:13-14).

Chapter Four

THE PROTECTION OF THE BLOOD

The tenth and final plague brought against the Egyptians which resulted in Israel's deliverance from the Pharaoh's rule was the Passover, or the death of the firstborn. Jehovah promised, "And all the firstborn in the land of Egypt shall die, from the firstborn of Pharaoh that sitteth upon his throne, even unto the firstborn of the maidservant that is behind the mill; and all the firstborn of beasts" (Exod. 11:5).

Even up to the dreadful ninth plague of locusts Pharaoh had repeatedly hardened his heart and refused to release the children of Israel. Each plague had grown worse and worse for the Egyptians. The death of the firstborn would be so great that God promised, " . . . there shall be *a great cry* throughout all the land of Egypt, such as there was none like it, nor shall be like it any more" (Exod. 11:6). The sorrow of this plague upon Pharaoh would cause the stubborn monarch to not only, "let you go, he shall surely thrust you out hence altogether" (Exod. 11:1).

God provided a way of escape from the plague for all who would believe the commandment and do according to His instructions. Note the relevance from the passage in Exodus 12 for us today.

Exodus 12:3—"Speak ye unto all the congregation of Israel, saying, In the tenth day of this month they shall take to them every man a lamb, according to the house of their fathers, a lamb for an house." It was each father's duty to provide a lamb for his family's protection.

Exodus 12:4—"And if the household be too little for the lamb, let him and *his neighbor next unto his house* take it according to the number of the souls; every man according to his eating shall make your count for the lamb." Sharing the lamb with his neighbor pictures the believer sharing the Lamb of God with his friends. After Christ told the Samaritan woman the secrets of her life she went into the city and said to the men, "Come, see a man, which told me all things that ever I did: is not this the Christ?" (John 4:29). The early Christians "(broke) bread from house to house . . . Praising God . . . And the Lord added to the church daily such as should be saved" (Acts 2:46-47).

Exodus 12:5—"Your lamb shall be without blemish, a male of the first year: ye shall take it out from the sheep, or from the goats." (Chapter 3, "Lamb Requirements" shows how Jesus perfectly fits this type.)

Exodus 12:6—"And ye shall keep it up until the fourteenth day of the same month: and the whole assembly of the congregation of Israel shall kill it in the evening." The last half of the time that Jesus was dying on the cross the first three Gospels all declare that a supernaturally created darkness hung over the land. "And it was about the sixth hour (noon), and there was a darkness over all the earth until the ninth hour (3 p.m.). And *the sun was darkened* . . . " (Luke 23:44-45; Matt. 27:45; Mark 15:33). Because God's Word states "the sun was darkened" we can draw from this implication that darkness surrounded the whole earth those three hours.

Exodus 12:7—"And they shall take of the blood, and strike it on the two *side* posts and on the *upper* door post of the houses, wherein they shall eat it." Notice, God did not mention the threshold of the door at all. Do not regard the blood of Christ as an unholy thing fit only to trample underfoot. Consider the following verse:

> "He that despised Moses' law died without mercy under two or three witnesses: Of how much sorer punishment, suppose ye, shall he be thought worthy, who hath trodden under foot the Son of God, and hath counted the blood of the covenant, wherewith he was sanctified, an unholy thing, and hath done despite unto the Spirit of grace?" (Heb. 10:28-29).

What does the above verse teach us?

FIRST: Those who reject the blood of the new covenant will suffer a "much sorer punishment" than those who despised Moses' law. The penalty for rejecting the law under the old covenant was "death without mercy" (see Numbers 15:30-31; Deuteronomy 17:2-6). The penalty for treading Jesus underfoot, counting the blood unholy, and despising the Holy Spirit is much sorer than physical death—it is an eternal death (see Revelation 21:8, 27).

SECOND: Just as the law despisers suffered death without mercy in the old covenant, there will be no mercy for those who die despising Jesus' sacrifice. "For we know him that hath said, Vengeance belongeth unto me, I will recompense, saith the Lord. And again, The Lord shall judge his people. It is a fearful thing to fall into the hands of the living God" (Heb. 10:30-31; see also 9:27; 12:35).

THIRD: This judgment will come on those who in time past "were sanctified." Notice, this mocker will be thought worthy of eternal punishment because he now counts the blood wherewith in time past he was sanctified an unholy, disgraceful thing. This would indicate that sanctified people can apostatize to a place of final rejection by God. At one time they did accept Christ's blood as their atonement, otherwise they could not have been sanctified by it. Later, through satanic influence, they completely disregarded (as common and unclean) Jesus' blood. When a person absolutely rejects Jesus' sacrifice, there remains no other sacrifice for sin (see Hebrews 10:26), and he will have to suffer punishment of such rejection.

A willful apostate, however, is different from a common backslider. The apostate rejects the truth that Christ's blood can save. As long as the backslider retains his faith in the atonement of Christ he can be renewed in repentance.

Exodus 12:8—"And they shall eat the flesh in that night, roast with fire, and unleavened bread; and with bitter herbs they shall eat it."

Exodus 12:9—"Eat not of it raw, nor sodden at all with water, but roast with fire; his head with his legs, and with the purtenance thereof." Eating the flesh of the passover lamb symbolizes eating the flesh (partaking of) Christ. Note John 6:52-58:

"The Jews therefore strove among themselves, saying, How can this man give us his flesh to eat? Then Jesus said unto them, Verily, verily, (truly, truly) I say unto you, Except ye eat the flesh of the Son of man, and drink his blood, ye have no life in you. Whoso eateth my flesh and drinketh my blood dwelleth in me, and I in him. As the living Father hath sent me, and I live by the Father: so he that eateth me, even he shall live by me. This is the bread which came down from heaven: not as your fathers did eat manna, and are dead: he that eateth of this bread shall live for ever."

Jesus was not a cannibal. There was no way the Jews who heard Him could take this statement to mean that. They knew from the Law that eating was figuratively used of partaking. In Proverbs 9:17 and Hosea 10:13 eating is spoken figuratively as partaking of evil. In the New Testament eating is used as one way of symbolically partaking of spiritual food. Paul says, "And did all eat the same spiritual meat" (1 Cor. 10:3). James speaks figuratively that cankered gold and silver shall "eat your flesh" (James 5:3). Christ spoke prophetically, "For the zeal of thine house hath eaten me up . . . " (Ps. 69:9). In John's vision he ate a book—"And I took the little book out of the angel's hand, and ate it up . . . " (Rev. 10:10).

Neither did Jesus mean that they must literally drink His blood. The Jews once again should have understood He meant they were to spiritually partake of His blood. They had no excuse to be offended at

His words. This figure of speech was common at the time. None of Jesus' followers took this statement literally for none of them (the women and John) at the foot of the cross drank His blood. This would have been an abomination in the sight of God for He has laid down a rule He has never revoked.

> "Moreover ye shall eat *no manner of blood* . . . whatsoever soul it be that eateth any manner of blood, even that soul shall be cut off from his people" (Lev. 7:26-27).

A clue to properly understanding what Jesus meant is seen in verse 51 of John 6: "I am the living bread . . . if any man eat of this bread, he shall live forever: and the bread that I will give is my flesh, which *I will give for the life of the world.*" Believing what He did upon the tree, then, would be partaking or eating of His flesh. In the act of giving His flesh for the life of the world He has provided His flesh and His blood for the believer to freely partake of. Christ instituted the "Lord's Supper" (see 1 Corinthians 11:20) that the church might partake of the elements of bread and wine (juice of the grape) and spiritually eat His flesh and drink His blood. Notice how Paul likens the communion to Israel's eating of the sacrifices:

> "The cup of blessing which we bless, is it not the communion of the blood of Christ? The bread which we break, is it not the communion of the body of Christ? For we being many are one bread, and one body: for we (the church) are *all partakers of that one bread (Christ).* Behold Israel after the flesh: are not they which *eat of the sacrifices* partakers of the altar?" (1 Cor.

10:16-18).

The communion (fellowship, sharing) of the blood and body are represented in the wine and bread. In John 6:51 Christ said, " . . . the bread . . . is my flesh . . . " Therefore eating His flesh is eating the bread which we bless in the Lord's Supper. Drinking His blood is drinking the juice in the cup which we bless. When a believer understands the Lord's Supper and partakes of the elements in faith there is a spiritual fellowship with the Lord and with fellow members of Christ's body. The blood of Christ and the flesh that bore stripes for our healing enters into the believer by the Spirit and is manifest in his mortal body. There is healing in the communion. Matthew's account of the Lord's Supper instituted at the last supper Christ ate with His disciples prior to the crucifixion is the most endearing to me of the four accounts in the New Testament. (See Matthew 26:26-30; Mark 14:22-25; Luke 22:14-20; 1 Corinthians 11:23-29.):

> "And as they were eating, *Jesus took bread*, and blessed it, and brake it, and gave it to the disciples, and said, Take, eat; *this is my body*. And he took the cup, and gave thanks, and gave it to them, saying, *Drink ye all of it*; For *this is my blood* of the new testament, which is shed for many for the remission of sins" (Matt. 26:26-30).

"As they were eating" points out the fact that the communion flowed naturally into being. It was not a starchy meeting, but a friendly and informal, communing in the love of God. "Jesus *took* bread, and *blessed* it, and *brake* it, and *gave* it . . . " He took, He blessed, He brake, and He gave. These four steps follow in progressive order in the lives of each of His disciples. He takes us into His arms when He saves us. He blesses us with the Holy Spirit. He breaks us at the cross. He gives us to others in ministry. We must experience the breaking of our self-life, however, before He can give us to His body as a ministry gift. We enjoy so much His taking and blessing of our lives.

Concerning the broken bread He said, "Take . . . " He gives but we must take what He gives. The broken bread represents the scourged and marred body offered for our healing (see Isaiah 53:5; 1 Peter 2:24). " . . . eat; this is my body." The bread eaten in faith ministers His flesh to us. He gave thanks for the cup saying, "Drink you all of it (everyone of you drink it); For this is my blood . . . " Do you follow His pattern of giving thanks for the cup by giving thanks to Him for His blood? Do you thank God for the blood of Christ? Notice in this text the two verbs indicating what each believer must do: eat and drink. The child of God must eat Christ's flesh and drink His blood.

The children of Israel were instructed to eat the flesh of that first passover lamb. They would begin their exodus (departure) that night and they needed the strength that lamb afforded. They were supernaturally strengthened and healed as they ate the roasted lamb. Behind closed doors, sprinkled with the blood, hundreds of thousands of Israelites partook of the flesh of the same lambs whose blood covered the respective homes in the land of Goshen. Under the covering of blood they hurriedly ate the flesh. Among these thousands throughout Goshen were hundreds of sick and diseased persons, yet a few hours later, " . . . there was not one feeble

41

(weak, sick) person among their tribes" (Ps. 105:37).*
The greatest mass miracle service that ever occurred
took place behind closed doors as the children of
Israel ate the lamb's flesh. The strength they received
from that one meal was so great that they traveled
"by day and night" for several days without ex-
haustion (see Exodus 13:21). When we partake by
faith of Jesus' flesh the same thing occurs today.
"For even Christ our passover (lamb) is sacrificed
for us" (1 Cor. 5:7).

They were to eat the lamb "roast(ed) with
fire . . . " Fire pictures God's acceptance of Christ as
in the Old Testament where fire showed God's
acceptance of the sacrifice. They were told not to
eat it raw (later all uncooked meats were forbidden); God was showing them the break the
Israelites must make with all the ways of Egypt. In
offering sacrifices to their idols the Egyptians often
ate raw meat. The Passover lamb was not to be "sodden (boiled) at all with water" since water is a type of

---

* Psalms 105:37 indicates that there was not one feeble (sick
or weak) person among the tribes of Israel who made the
exodus, yet there was a law given regarding lepers. Many of
those who came out of Egypt strong and healthy got sick
during the waters of Marah only a few days later (see Exodus
15:23-26), but then God established His healing covenant
with Israel (Exodus 15:26) which taught if one did not walk
in obedience he could be afflicted. Miriam made the exodus
from Egypt and danced on the Red Sea shore (Exodus 15:20-
21) and was not weak or diseased at that time, yet later in
life criticized Moses and was struck with leprosy (Numbers
12:1-15). Just because everyone was healthy in Egypt (Goshen
does not mean they would always stay well. They could become ill through rebellion, murmuring, unbelief, or disobedience, etc., and is comparable with John 5:14.

42

ife and the Perfect Lamb tasted death.

Unleavened Bread

They were to eat the flesh with unleavened bread. We are to partake of the Lamb with purity, sincerity, and truth. It is most important to see in the Word what leaven represents. Leaven typifies iniquity, false doctrine, hypocrisy, and uncleanness.

First: Leaven bread was never to be offered in a blood sacrifice. "Thou shalt not offer the blood of my sacrifice with leavened bread . . . " (Exod. 23:18).

Second: No burnt offering was to be made with leaven. "No meat offering, which ye shall bring unto the LORD, shall be made with leaven: for ye shall burn no leaven, nor any honey, in any offering of the LORD made by fire" (Lev. 2:11). When Israel was hot with adultery the Lord likened it to leavened bread baked in an oven. "They are all adulterers, as an oven heated by the baker, who ceaseth from raising after he hath kneaded the dough, until it be leavened" (Hos. 7:4). Leaven typifies lust.

Third: Jesus pictured the corruption of the kingdom in this age to the fermentation of leaven. "Another parable spake he unto them; The kingdom of heaven is like unto leaven, which a woman took, and hid in three measures of meal, till the whole was leavened" (Matt. 13:33; see also Luke 13:21). He was showing by this parable that the church age would be filled with false doctrine and impurity that would pollute the truth and ministry of the kingdom. As false doctrine began to enter the church toward the end of the first century A.D. it grew and multiplied until at this hour we can easily observe "the whole (is) leavened." Paul warned the church at Galatia that the hindering persuasion of false doctrine they were accepting was not from God. He reminded the early Christians, "A little leaven leaveneth the whole lump" (Gal. 5:9).

On this same line Jesus warned His disciples, "Take heed and beware of the leaven of the Pharisees and of the Sadducees" (Matt. 16:6). The disciples, whose hearts were hardened, misunderstood Christ. They reasoned among themselves, " . . . It is because we have taken no bread" (v. 7). Jesus told them, "I spake it not to you concerning bread . . . " (v. 11). "Then understood they how that He bade them not beware of the leaven of bread, but of *the doctrine of the Pharisees and of the Sadducees*" (v. 12). Leaven speaks figuratively of false doctrine which we are to "beware of" (see also Mark 8:14-21).

Our Lord's fourth truth illustrated by leaven concerns hypocrisy. "In the mean time, when there were gathered together an innumerable multitude of people, insomuch that they trode one upon another, he began to say unto his disciples first of all, Beware ye of the leaven of the Pharisees, *which is hypocrisy*. For there is nothing covered, that shall not be revealed; neither hid, that shall not be known" (Luke 12:1-2). Religious play-acting is also symbolized by leaven. Churches today are filled with such leaven in their so-called "worship services" during which they follow a printed program rather than the moving of the Holy Spirit.

Fifth, the church of Corinth was infected with uncleanness that even the heathen had no name for. A man living with his father's wife! Rather than mourning over this sad condition and seeking to rectify it, the Corinthians were puffed up (see 1 Corinthians 5:1-5). As Paul ministers the necessary church discipline he rebukes them saying, "Your glorying is not good. Know ye not that a little leaven leaveneth the whole lump? Purge out therefore the old leaven, that ye may be a new lump, as ye are unleavened. For even Christ our passover is sacrificed for us: Therefore let us keep the feast, not with old leaven, neither with the leaven of malice and wickedness; but with the unleavened bread of sincerity and truth" (vs. 6-8). " . . . the leaven of malice and wickedness," sad to say, is prevalent within the ranks of the church in this final hour. If we do not obey the command "to purge out . . . the old leaven" we will not be "a new lump" the Master will honor. Leaven represents evil and sin. Observe that Israel could not eat the lamb without unleavened bread. Neither can the believer partake of·Christ while holding to false doctrine, hypocrisy, and sin. We must purge ourselves from these that we might feast at His table. "Let every one that nameth the name of Christ depart from iniquity" (2 Tim. 2:19).

Exodus 12:10—"And ye shall let nothing of it remain until the morning; and that which remaineth of it until the morning ye shall burn with fire." This teaches us that there is a limited time that the Christian may experience God and when it is over ("when the morning dawns") it is over! " . . . after this the judgment" (Heb. 9:27).

Exodus 12:11—"And thus shall ye eat it; with your loins girded, your shoes on your feet, and your staff in your hand; and ye shall eat it in haste: it is the LORD'S passover." The first part of this verse corresponds with the believer's "whole armour of

God" by which our loins are to be girt, our feet are to be shod, etc. (see Ephesians 6:10-18). The admonition to "eat it in haste" pictures for us to get all of God while we can. "Seek ye the LORD while he may be found, call ye upon him while he is near" (Isa. 55:6). "For he will finish the work, and cut it short in righteousness: because a short work will the Lord make upon the earth" (Rom. 9:28). Be ready to leave!

Pass As A Guard

Exodus 12:12—"For I will pass through the land of Egypt this night, and will smite all the firstborn, both man and beast; and against all the gods of Egypt I will execute judgment: I am the LORD." It appears from this verse that the Lord does the actual smiting upon the firstborn. Looking in verse 23 however, we see there are two different beings that will pass through the land. One who PROTECTS; the other who DESTROYS. "For the LORD will pass through to smite the Egyptians; and when he seeth the blood upon the lintel, and on the two side posts, the LORD will pass (as a guard) over the door, and will not suffer (permit, allow) the destroyer to come in unto your houses to smite you." Notice the Lord guards over the blood-sprinkled door and does not permit the destroyer to come in the house to smite the oldest child. Here we see that two persons swept through the land that memorial night. The Lord is the protector. Who is referred to as "the destroyer?" Jesus gives us the answer in John 10:10. "The thief cometh not, but for to steal, and to kill, and *to destroy*. I am come that they might have life, and that they might have it more abundantly." Satan (the thief) comes to destroy. The devil is the destroyer.

(See footnote at end of this chapter).

The Blood Token

Exodus 12:13-22—"And the blood shall be to you for a token upon the houses where ye are: and when I see the blood, I will pass over you, and the plague shall not be upon you to destroy you, when I smite the land of Egypt. . . . And ye shall take a bunch of hyssop, and dip it in the blood that is in the basin, and strike the lintel and the two side posts with the blood that is in the basin; and none of you shall go out of the door of his house until the morning." If an Israelite followed the instructions to cover his doorway with the blood at the top and the sides the Lord passed as a protector. And the plague the destroyer brought with him was not upon the Israelite house. It is interesting to note that the Egyptians were not even instructed concerning the blood covering. Pharaoh, their ruler, typifies the god of this world who has no propitiation and therefore despises those who do. Today Satan and the fallen angels have no covering in Jesus' blood. "For verily he took not on him the nature of angels; but he took on him the seed of Abraham" (Heb. 2:16). The word *token* means evidence, sign. The blood was a sign on the houses; an evidence of divine protection. The devil could not touch that which was covered by the blood. The blood sheltered the firstborn from certain death. Without the blood, death was inevitable. Covered by the blood, protection was guaranteed.

There was one condition the blood-covered must meet. They were not permitted to go out of their homes! " . . . none of you shall go out at the door of his house until the morning." Although we have

47

perfect present protection from the enemy at this time we can forfeit our claim to divine covering if we do not "abide in him; that when he shall appear, we may have confidence, and not be ashamed before him at his coming" (1 John 2:28). Many would like to think they are immune to satanic attack due to their "hedge." The Bible warns and informs, " . . . whoso breaketh an hedge, a serpent shall bite him" (Eccl. 10:8). We do have a protective hedge and covering in Jesus' blood which Satan cannot trespass. If we do not "walk in the light as He is in the light" the "blood of Jesus Christ His Son" does not "cleanse us from all sin" (see 1 John 1:7). Our present protection can be removed by walking in any darkness at all. This reveals why holiness is a must (see Hebrews 12:14). Many years later the spies instructed Rahab to "bind this line of scarlet thread in the window" as the *true token* she had requested of them. The "scarlet line" was the sign of redemption to the invading Hebrew army a few days later and they spared Rahab and all who were in her house from destruction (see Joshua 2, 6). The Israelites knew that scarlet was symbolic for blood (see Leviticus 14:4). Just as they had been spared in the land of Egypt by blood covering they were to "save alive" any who abode in the house of the harlot who had trusted by faith in the scarlet thread (see Hebrews 11:31). The "blood line" concept is based upon this passage in Joshua chapter two. The Israelites were blood conscious and passed this blood consciousness on to a heathen prostitute in Jericho. Today the blood of Christ is for all who come to God. All are saved from certain destruction by the blood of Jesus.

Accepting The Blood By Faith

During the time that the head of each household was applying the blood to the doorway of his home, the firstborn of the family was inside the house and remained there until morning. He was on the inside; the blood was applied to the outside door frame. He was not allowed to stick his head outside even once. This meant he could not see the blood that covered him. Neither can we see by natural sight the blood that covers us. The firstborn had to accept by faith that he was covered by the blood. We must accept by faith what our Father has done for us. I can imagine the oldest son asking, "Dad, are you sure you applied the blood just as Moses said to?" When an affirmative reply came the son had to rely only on the integrity of his father's word. So must we. The firstborn could not see the blood nor feel the blood but he was covered just the same. "For we walk by faith, not by sight" (2 Cor. 5:7).

Satan was not working in the interest of Israel when he destroyed the firstborn of man and beast on the Passover night. Satan hates all mankind and wanted to destroy the firstborn of Israel as well as Egypt, but was prevented in doing so because the angel of the Lord stood as a guard over the blood-sprinkled doorways. Had a Hebrew family not applied the blood to the door of their home their oldest son would have been destroyed. If it would seem contradictory that the Lord would use Satan in the accomplishment of His purposes remember that "The Lord hath made all things for himself; yea, even the wicked for the day of evil" (Prov. 16:4). When Saul rebelled against God, " . . . an evil spirit from the Lord troubled him" (1 Sam. 16:14). God permitted an evil spirit to trouble Saul because "rebellion is as the sin of witchcraft" (1 Sam. 15:23). God withdrew His protective hand, and the evil spirit came in. Even in the New Testament church, in dealing with a need for church discipline, the fornicator was turned "over to Satan for the destruction of the flesh" (1 Cor. 5:5).

Chapter Five

JUSTIFICATION BY THE BLOOD

"Much more then, being now justified by his blood, we shall be saved from wrath through him" (Rom. 5:9). We are justified (just-as-if-I'd-never sinned) upon the basis of the blood of Christ. Justification by the blood is a new covenant truth and reality for us today who accept Jesus. The New Testament and the grace of God is substance, whereas the Old Testament and the law of God is a shadow. "For the law having a shadow (outline) of good things to come (the new covenant) . . . " (Heb. 10:1). "Which are a shadow of things to come; but the body is of Christ" (Col. 2:17). This new and living way that Jesus has consecrated for us can be seen typically in the law. The law foreshadows and gives insight into the work that Christ has accomplished for us.

Leviticus 14:1-7 is only one sentence and yet completely pictures the death and resurrection of our Lord Jesus Christ:

"And the LORD spake unto Moses, saying,
(2) This shall be the law of the leper in the day of his cleansing: He shall be brought

unto the priest: (3) And the priest shall go forth out of the camp; and the priest shall look, and, behold, if the plague of leprosy be healed in the leper; (4) Then shall the priest command to take for him that is to be cleansed two birds alive and clean, and cedar wood, and scarlet, and hyssop: (5) And the priest shall command that one of the birds be killed in an earthen vessel over running water: (6) As for the living bird, he shall take it, and the cedar wood, and the scarlet, and the hyssop, and shall dip them and the living bird in the blood of the bird that was killed over the running water: (7) And he shall sprinkle upon him that is to be cleansed from the leprosy seven times, and shall pronounce him clean, and shall let the living bird loose into the open field."

When God puts seven verses in one sentence He is showing us there is one main thought in it. Many principles can be seen from this one section of Scripture but one primary truth comes from it.

In order to understand the spiritual truths contained in this passage it is important to first explain the natural procedure of what happened here. "Howbeit that was not first which is spiritual, but that which is natural; and afterward that which is spiritual" (1 Cor. 15:46). First we will study the natural order of events and then proceed to discover the spiritual truth.

A leper was a man who was unclean, and due to his leprosy was put outside of fellowship with God's people—outside the camp. Wherever Israel was journeying in the wilderness they camped and outside the main camp the excluded leper abode in a separate tent. Even though he was an Israelite the leprosy made him unclean.

God provided a cleansing for the leper. After the plague was healed the leper had to be ceremonially cleansed before coming back into the camp. The priest went outside the camp into an open field near a running stream. With him he brought two living birds that were clean according to the law. He also brought a piece of cedar wood, a small scarlet cloth, and a hyssop branch. In addition to these items he carried an earthen vessel, or a clay pot as we say today. The head of one bird was pulled off inside this earthen vessel as it was held over the running water (stream). Then the living bird, the wood, the cloth, and the branch were dipped in the blood of the dead bird. After this the priest sprinkled blood with the hyssop branch seven times on the leper. The man was pronounced "Clean" and, finally, the living bird was released to fly into the air still wet and dripping with the former bird's blood.

Consider for a moment the great obedience that is exhibited in the Old Testament sacrifices. To the natural minds of the priests, how foolish and without meaning these and other events seemed. There was no logical reasoning or explanation for all these details. Yet without hesitation, the priests obeyed year after year the exact directions given them. They did not have the revelation of what they were doing as we have it today. Throughout the Word of God we see many instances where God instructed a person, or a people, to do certain things which to the natural mind seemed senseless. (Imagine how Peter felt when the Lord told him to get the tax money from opening a fish's mouth!)

Do not dismiss the details of this or any sacrifice as mere ritualism as the liberals have. Jesus said, "Man shall . . . live by . . . every word that proceedeth out of the mouth of God" (Matt. 4:4). Prophetically Christ speaks, " . . . in the volume of the book it is written of me" (Ps. 40:7). Jesus is on every page of the Bible. Let's notice the spiritual truths of this beautiful passage in Leviticus.

"This shall be the law of the leper in the day of his cleansing . . . " It only takes a day for a leper to be cleansed. Leprosy is a type of sin. We all were sinners. It only took a day to be cleansed from our sin in the blood of Christ! (see Zechariah 3:9). The priest "goes out of the camp" which shows us that our Great High Priest in making atonement for us, "suffered without (outside) the gate" (Heb. 13:12). Jesus went outside of the gates of the city of Jerusalem in order to cleanse us. Next we come to the two birds which also symbolize Christ. He is both the priest and the birds in this passage. Why two living birds? One could be killed to symbolize the crucified Christ. The other left alive is to picture the resurrected Christ. One alone could not be killed and resurrected. That is the reason God commanded to take two birds. The second bird was only released after this first bird had been slain. The second bird was released in the blood of the first bird. The resurrected Christ sprinkled His own blood on the mercy seat before the Father in heaven following His resurrection.

Notice the two characteristics of the birds. Alive and clean. *Alive:* Pilate testified, " . . . nothing worthy of death is done unto Him" (Luke 23:15). Jesus was alive and worthy of life. He had never sinned and was not worthy of sin's punishment: death. Death was totally contradictory to the nature of Jesus Christ. He *was* life (see John 14:6). *Clean:* " . . . who knew no sin" (2 Cor. 5:21). He was separate from sin, holy and blameless. Because He was clean He had the right to remain alive.

The cedar wood symbolizes the cross. Cross in the New Testament is the word *stauros* which means straight pole, stake, or post set upright. This is important because it brings forth the idea of hanging on *a tree*.* Cedar wood is common in the near east. We cannot say for sure but perhaps it was on cedar wood that our Lord was nailed. Anyway, the cedar wood was dipped in the blood of the dead bird and the cross was drenched with the blood of Christ.

The scarlet was a red cloth. Scarlet pictures blood. Cloth pictures covering. " . . . it is the blood that maketh an atonement (covering) for the soul" (Lev. 17:11). This scarlet cloth was red, wet with blood. Hyssop is a branch that is not very strong. It cannot support a heavy weight but was suitable for sprinkling blood. "And ye shall take a bunch of hyssop, and dip it in the blood that is in the basin,

---

Tree is translated timber and is not the same Greek word as cross. It is used in 1 Peter 2:24; Acts 5:30; and Galatians 3:13. Jesus used this very word on the way to Golgotha in Luke 23:31. See also Deuteronomy 21:22-23. The idea we are bringing forth is that Jesus was crucified on a timber pole such as the trunk of a tree and not on a conventional-looking cross which was in fact conceived by religious tradition. The cross our Saviour hung on looked enough like a tree as to be rendered such at least four times in Scripture.

and strike the lintel and the two side posts with the blood that is in the basin . . . " (Exod. 12:22). It was with the hyssop that the blood was transferred from the basin to the door post. The blood was applied with hyssop. Hyssop was also used to sprinkle water. "And a clean person shall take hyssop, and dip it in water, and sprinkle it upon the tent . . . " (Num. 19:18). Notice that a person first had to be clean before he could sprinkle water. By the sprinkling of blood a person is made clean and fit to sprinkle water. What does this water represent? "Christ also loved the church, and gave himself for it; that he might sanctify and cleanse it with the washing of water by the word . . . " (Eph. 5:25-26). After we have been made clean by Christ's blood we are in a position to be further set apart to the Father by the Word. Jesus prayed, "Sanctify them through thy truth: thy word is truth" (John 17:17). Through Ezekiel God promised, "Then will I sprinkle clean water upon you, and you shall be clean: from all your filthiness, and from your idols, will I cleanse you" (Ezek. 36:25). Hyssop represents faith. It is by faith that the blood is obtained and maintained. It is by faith that we apply the Word of God to our lives.

As "kings and priests" and as the "royal priesthood" the believer is able to sprinkle Jesus' blood (see Revelation 1:5-6; 1 Peter 2:9). As the head of his home a father can apply the blood to his family, just as the father applied the blood to his doorposts in Exodus chapter twelve. Then the head of the household can sprinkle water over his family or teach them the Word of God. Jesus demonstrated this principle when He cleansed His disciples by His spoken word. "Now ye are clean through the word which I have spoken unto you" (John 15:3). David prayed, "Purge me with hyssop, and I shall be clean: wash me, and I shall be whiter than snow" (Ps. 51:7).

The earthen vessel pictures the body of humiliation that the Word (Jesus) walked in. The bird was killed IN the earthen vessel. Jesus died in His body. Jesus gave the life of His flesh for the world. His body was created by a supernatural act of God in the womb of the virgin. However, it was a natural body like yours and mine. *Earthen* pictures clay. This speaks of a natural body made of the dust of the ground. He became actual flesh. "We have this treasure in earthen vessels . . . " (2 Cor. 4:7). Jesus Christ is in us. Although His body was natural it was perfect without sin or disease. Jesus lived in perfect health. As the Word was entering earth's atmosphere He spoke back to the Father gazing upon the womb He would shortly enter, "Wherefore when he cometh into the world, he saith, Sacrifice and offering (the blood of bulls and goats) Thou wouldest not (desired no more), but *a body hast Thou prepared me* (to offer the perfect sacrifice with)" (Heb. 10:5). " . . . we are sanctified through the BODY of Jesus Christ once for all" (Heb. 10:10). As the Holy Spirit formed that embryo in the womb of Mary the Word entered into it.

Earthen also means frail. In our present bodies there is no way we can experience the fullness of God's presence. We need a glorified body for that!

Now we come to the running water which was a flowing stream out in the open field. The earthen vessel was held over the running water while the first bird was killed. What does this tell us?

"How much more shall the blood of Christ, who through *the eternal Spirit* offered himself without spot to God, purge your conscience from dead works to serve the living God?" (Heb. 9:14).

Running water is the shadow. "The eternal Spirit" is the substance. Running corresponds to eternal; Water is often a type of the Holy Spirit. Water is used as a symbol of the Holy Spirit more than anything else in the Scriptures. Just as the blood of the bird was shed over running water, the blood of Christ was offered through the eternal Spirit. As the blood was shed on the cross, the Holy Spirit offered up the work of Christ before the Father. Three days later the Holy Spirit (see Romans 1:4) raised up or quickened the body and Jesus presented Himself to the Father that day (see John 20:17). The conscience is the voice of the human spirit. Our conscience is purged by the blood of Christ and the demands of righteousness are satisfied. The spirit is made alive to serve and worship the living God.

The reason the priest sprinkled the leper seven times is that seven is the Bible number for perfection or completeness. Seven is used over and over to show this. When we are initially cleansed by the blood all our sins are washed away and we are made completely clean. The Father agrees with the sacrifice of Christ and we are pronounced clean at the very throne of God. The legal demands of sin are met and in the judicial mind of God a change in regard to us occurs. He pronounces us clean, clothes us with righteousness, and gives us eternal life. All of this occurs in the throne room.

Here on earth the Spirit bears witness to our

spirit that we are a child of God. We have passed from death to life. Justification is pronounced from the throne before regeneration occurs in the human spirit. This is how one is accepted in "the beloved" —our Lord Jesus Christ. We are admitted into fellowship with God and His people and are no longer excluded from "the camp."

The living bird, dipped in the blood of the dead bird, is released into the open field. The bird takes wings and flies off into the sky. The resurrected Christ dipped Himself in the blood of His sacrifice and presented His blood to the Father, and "obtained eternal redemption for us" (Heb. 9:12).

Chapter Six

SANCTIFICATION BY THE BLOOD

Our next study on the blood of Christ brings us to verse 14 of Leviticus fourteen. We saw in verses 1-7 cleansing for the leper. No longer is he referred to as a leper after verse seven, for he has been pronounced clean. Yet only seven days after this pronouncement he returns to the priest for a further cleansing once more through the sprinkling of blood.

No longer are we sinners, yet further cleansing is needed. This pictures the truth that a believer is justified and pronounced clean at conversion. Desiring to be made perfect he returns to his Great High Priest for a deeper cleansing. The seven days lapsing between the first and second cleansing pictures the desire for perfection in the heart of one whose desire is to be perfect even as His Father in heaven is perfect (see Matthew 5:48). Seven is the number of perfection.

In verse eight the leper is allowed to leave his tent and come into the camp. No longer is he excluded as a leper from fellow Israelites. We are brought into "fellowship with one another" after we are justified (see 1 John 1:7). Another benefit of justification is represented by the washing of water in verse nine. " . . . he shall wash his clothes, also he shall wash his flesh in water . . . " After our (verse seven) experience of justification we are permitted, even commanded, to employ "the washing of water by the word" (Eph. 5:26). On the eighth day after the leper has been pronounced clean from leprosy he is permitted to go to the priest at the door of the tabernacle (verse eleven). There he offers sacrifice to the Lord. Two he lambs and one ewe lamb without blemish are sacrificed as a sin, trespass, and burnt offering. A log of oil is waved before the Lord for a wave offering. This brings us to the focal point of this chapter's study:

> "And the priest shall take some of the blood of the trespass offering, and the priest shall put it upon the tip of the right ear of him that is to be cleansed, and upon the thumb of his right hand, and upon the great toe of his right foot" (Lev. 14:14).

Why was the blood in each case put upon the right side of the man to be cleansed? The right side throughout the Word is the side of divine favor. Examples: The sheep will go on His right, the goats on His left. Jesus is seated at the right hand of God. Jesus stretched forth His right hand and laid it upon John's shoulder, etc. You are never on the wrong side when you deal with the blood. It's right!

Remember that the law is a shadow and the new covenant is the substance. The ear, hand, and foot in the law symbolize the believer's thought life, ministry, and fellowship. Jesus was our substitute in these areas of our life.

The Passover Lamb's body was opened as a fountain for sin (see Zechariah 13:1) in five principle areas. In the order they occurred, the blood flowed from His back, His head, His hands, His feet, and His side. The blood flowed from His back for our healing and from His side for our infilling of the Holy Spirit. The three places in between were opened for our sanctification in the same corresponding realms of life. As the Roman soldiers forcibly platted the crown of thorns the blood flowed from His head to sanctify our minds. The blood of the trespass offering was put on the tip of the right ear of him that was to be cleansed symbolizing the blood of Christ sanctifying all that enters our thought life. The blood was put on the thumb of the former leper's right hand symbolizing the blood of Christ sanctifying our works in the kingdom of God. Jesus' hands were nailed for this purpose. The blood was put upon the Israelite's great toe that the precious blood might be upon our walk with the Father. Jesus' feet were nailed that ours might walk. Unrestricted fellowship is enjoyed with the Father through the blood of the Son.

Do not let the term "sanctification" scare you. The verb "sanctify" means to set apart and to make clean. Sanctification is the process of being separated and made clean unto God. A primary purpose of Jesus' suffering for us was to accomplish this cleansing aspect in the lives of His people. "Wherefore Jesus also, that he might sanctify the people with his own blood, suffered without (outside) the gate" (Heb. 13:12). Jesus is the sanctifier, the people are the object of His sanctifying grace, the blood is the means of cleansing, or the sanctifying agent.

61

The Thought Life

The first area of cleansing for the former leper is the ear. We need the blood on what we hear. How well David knew the distracting voice of the enemy! "I am restless in my complaint and am surely distracted, because of the voice of the enemy . . . " (Ps. 55:2-3 NASB). Many are distracted from spiritual devotion due to satanic interference. Others find their minds assaulted by an obsession of demonized thoughts. The blood of Christ provides the legal basis for victory in the believer's thought life.

As our great substitute, the Man who never had an evil thought (although He did have thoughts of evil) transferred His pure mind to us by His blood.* "We have the mind of Christ," and freedom from slavery to sin in our thoughts (1 Cor. 2:16). Our ear is set apart to God picturing that the disciple can hear His Master's voice. Our Substitute took all our wicked imaginations when He was offered as sin to God. He never had mental wickedness yet He took ours and gave us mental purity in its place.

For thirty-three years Jesus walked in a natural body and was subject to all the temptations we are.

---

* Our Lord Jesus Christ never had an evil thought. He was "undefiled" (Hebrews 7:26) and He said, "Evil thoughts . . . defile the man" (see Mark 7:20-23). Had He had one evil thought He would have been defiled. This is not to say He had no thought of or from (the) evil (one). The difference is that an evil thought "comes from within" while a thought of evil comes from an outside source (the tempter). A thought of evil turns into an evil thought if the will of the mind accepts what has come from without. Jesus' will always delighted in doing the will of God thus the thoughts of the evil one were repelled. Jesus was tempted in His thoughts but never yielded in His mind.

Satan attempted to flash vile pictures across His thought processes. Not once did Jesus entertain and give place to a thought from the evil one. On the other hand, the sinner harbored evil imaginations and toyed with vile thoughts from an early age. Jesus was never polluted in His mind and by the wonder of substitutions provides a holy mind for all who believe. He puts the blood on our mind in the same manner that the priest put the blood on the tip of the right ear. Our mind is separated unto God and made a holy receptacle of God's Word. When our thoughts are fixed on Him we have perfect peace on the basis of His blood.

You can silence the voice of the accuser by testifying openly the merits of Jesus' blood. "And they overcame him (the accuser) by the blood of the Lamb, and by the word of their testimony (vocal agreement); and they loved not their lives unto the death (their wills were fully fixed on the Father's will)" (Rev. 12:11).

All the divine revelation, enlightenment, and illumination the Christian receives comes from the Holy Spirit through the Word on the basis and legal ground of the blood. As a priest in the kingdom of God you are privileged to sprinkle with His blood. The phrase "plead the blood of Jesus" is not actually in the Bible but the principle is taught in many places where different individuals sprinkled the blood upon people or even places (Leviticus 14:25; Hebrews 9:21).

All the Christian's material possessions are under the protection of the blood. The firstborn of the beasts did not die if the owner sprinkled the blood upon the door of his home (see Exodus 12).

63

The blood of Jesus is a weapon of our warfare, but we must use it daily to enjoy the benefits derived therefrom.

The Believer's Works

Next, the blood was applied to the thumb of the right hand. What does the hand picture in the Word of God? Consider the following Scriptures:

"And Jesus said unto him, No man, having put his hand to the plough, and looking back, is fit for (the ministry of) the kingdom of God" (Luke 9:62).

"And these signs shall follow them that believe; In my name . . . they shall lay hands on the sick, and they shall recover" (Mark 16:17-18).

"Whatsoever thy hand findeth to do, do it with thy might . . . " (Eccl. 9:10).

"And let the beauty of the LORD our God be upon us: and establish Thou the works of our hands upon us; yea, the work of our hands establish thou it" (Ps. 90:17).

In these passages hands can be compared to works. Our works in the church are the same as our particular ministries in the body of Christ. Sowing and reaping are both operations effected by the hand in actual farming. Sowing the Word and reaping the harvest is the mission of the believer (cf. Psalm 126:6). Our ministry is effective with the blood sprinkled upon it, and ineffectual apart from the blood. Unconfessed sin allows Satan to bind our hands so that our ministry is not functioning properly.

Consider your works prior to salvation. Your hands framed wickedness and worked deceit. Consider Jesus' hands. For 33 years He did nothing wrong at all; His works were all holy. The first thirty years His hands were employed in the art of carpentry. He made beautiful objects from raw materials. He built tables, chairs, and other needful articles. He never stole or destroyed another's property. After the wilderness experience He returned to Galilee in the power of the Spirit laying hands on the sick, breaking and multiplying bread and fish, raising fallen people, and doing good. His hands did not deserve the nails, but by the blood that flowed from His hands He has cleansed ours from their former filth and set them apart for the work of God.

Every good work and deed performed by the Christian is acceptable to God as a pleasing sacrifice only because of the blood of Christ. When we lay our hands on the sick, the devil flees. The author committed many acts of sin by which Satan employed his hands for the advancement of darkness. These very hands are today used by God. It is all by the sanctifying grace afforded by Jesus and His blood. "Blessed be the LORD my strength, which teacheth my hands to war, and my fingers to fight" (Ps. 144:1).

When the enemy begins to interfere with your works and ministry overcome his binding attacks by confessing the merits of the blood against him (see James 4:7). As a member of the royal priesthood you can sprinkle the blood on your ministry.

Our Walk With God

The third place the blood was applied to him that was to be cleansed was upon the great (big) toe of his right foot. This corresponds to the area of fellowship with God. Notice the connection between walking and fellowship: "But if we *walk* in the light, as he is in the light, we have *fellowship* one with another, and the blood of Jesus Christ his Son cleanseth (and keeps on cleansing) us from all sin" (1 John 1:7). If we walk with God we have fellowship. The blood of Jesus Christ provides a basis for continual fellowship by continual cleansing. God is of purer eyes than to behold evil and cannot look with favor on iniquity (see Habakkuk 1:13).

Although we were initially cleansed at salvation further cleansing is needed as the years go by because God cannot fellowship with us when sin is present in our lives. All of us at sometime miss the mark and must confess our sin that the blood may be applied. Without confession of sin there is no application of the blood (see 1 John 1:9). God's ideal for us is "that ye sin not" (1 John 2:1-2), but has made adequate provision for uncleanness in the Christian's life in the meritorious sacrifice of Christ.

The most enjoyable aspect of the new life is fellowship with God. Our feet may stay in step with God when set apart by the blood that we may get to know the Father intimately.

The Oil On The Blood

This study would not be complete without verse 17 of Leviticus 14. Immediately after verse 14 the topic turns from blood to oil:

"And the priest shall take some of the log

66

of oil, and pour it into the palm of his own left hand: And the priest shall dip his right finger in the oil that is in his left hand, and shall sprinkle of the oil with his finger seven times before the LORD: And of the rest of the oil that is in his hand shall the priest put upon the tip of the right ear of him that is to be cleansed, and upon the thumb of his right hand, and upon the great toe of his right foot, *upon the blood* of the trespass offering" (Lev. 14:15-17).

It goes without saying that oil is usually a type of the Holy Spirit. All students of the Word agree at this point. The oil was sprinkled seven times before the Lord, showing that the Spirit proceeds to us from the Father. Jesus verbalized this truth in John 15:26, "But when the Comforter is come, whom I will send unto you from the Father, even the Spirit of truth, which proceedeth from the Father, he shall testify of me."

The rest of the oil in the priest's hand was put in the same spot on the man that the blood had been put only a few moments previously. The Lord instructed, " . . . put the oil . . . upon the blood . . . " Put the oil on the blood. Where the blood was not, the oil was not. The priest anointed the Israelite with oil only after he was touched by blood. It is true today that the Lord anoints us with the fresh oil of the Holy Spirit only after we are covered by the blood of Christ. If we honor the blood, God will honor us with the Holy Spirit working in our behalf. The thought life is inspired as the oil is put on the ear. Our ministry is empowered afresh as the Holy Spirit quickens. Our fellowship with God is enriched as the Comforter communicates between the Father and His children. We hear God's voice, work the works of God, and walk with the Father as the Spirit enables. Charles Wesley had this revelation of the oil after the blood when he sang, "The Spirit answers to the blood." When there is a lack of the anointing examine yourself in regard to the blood. The blood is the legal basis of authority; the Holy Spirit does the actual empowering.

The Full Anointing

After the Israelite was anointed in the three specific areas the oil was poured all over his head and coursed down his garments. "And the remnant of the oil that is in the priest's hand he shall pour upon the head of him that is to be cleansed: and the priest shall make an atonement for him before the LORD" (Lev. 14:18). This represents the fullness of the Spirit upon the believer. All he does is anointed with the Holy Spirit. How beautiful to walk in this measure of the overall anointing!

Chapter Seven

THE COSTLY SACRIFICE

The concept of making a sacrifice in the minds of most believers today is to give up something of value, or endure something of hardness. This concept formed in our thinking due to the biblical procedure of sacrificing to God. When Araunah freely offered King David the threshingfloor and the oxen to sacrifice unto the Lord, David replied, "Nay: but I will surely buy it of thee at a price: neither will I offer burnt offerings unto the LORD my God of that which cost me nothing" (2 Sam. 24:24). A sacrifice which cost the sacrificer nothing was not a sacrifice. Ancient Israel searched out the best of the flocks and would pay the owner a suitable price. Then he would bring the animal unto the priest to offer unto the Lord.

The most costly sacrifice in the Old Testament was Solomon's personal offering. Never before had Israel seen a greater sacrifice in terms of material cost. We are told this in 1 Kings 8:62-64:

"And the king, and all Israel with him,
offered sacrifice before the LORD. And

Solomon offered a sacrifice of peace offering, which he offered unto the LORD, *two and twenty thousand oxen, and an hundred and twenty thousand sheep*. So the king and all the children of Israel dedicated the house of the LORD. The same day did the king hallow the middle of the court that was before the house of the LORD: for there he offered burnt offerings, and meat offerings, and the fat of the peace offerings: because the brasen altar that was before the LORD was *too little to receive* the burnt offerings, and meat offerings, and the fat of the peace offerings."

It is hard to imagine the actual cost of such a huge sacrifice. In that time their measure of material values were much different from ours. By our standard of measurement it would probably cost more than $10 million to buy these animals on the open market. By their material standards this was worth even much more than it would be to us today.

The blood of these sacrifices would measure into the millions of gallons. The blood from one oxen would overflow the average bathtub. Twenty-two thousand oxen were offered. One hundred and twenty thousand sheep would make a sea of white in a huge field. It staggers the imagination to think how great and large this offering actually was. It was so large, in fact, that the large brazen altar was "too little to receive" the offerings. The middle of the court (the entire area where the altar was) became the place of sacrifice. We are not told how many priests were busy at work, or how long it took to offer these sacrifices. One thing is for certain: it took hours and hours!

Most of the Israelites had never seen as much livestock in their lifetime. Each of God's ancient people were doing well to sacrifice an occasional lamb. This sacrifice was never equaled in Israel's history. The modernists of today would regard this sacrifice as one huge waste. Even the moderates would question, "Would not one animal provide the necessary blood requirement?" For the law contained no commandment to offer such an army of flocks and herds.

While meditating on this passage the Holy Spirit gave the author an insight into this unusual event. *Solomon was sacrificing by a revelation!* He foresaw the inestimable cost of the perfect Lamb required by God. Jesus is God's Lamb. The Father searched out the best of heaven for second-best would not do. Only the Anointed One in His bosom would qualify for the title, "The Lamb of God." Such was not an ordinary lamb, nor an ordinary man. The Word sent from heaven became flesh and dwelt among us and we beheld His glory! (see John 1:14). Solomon's costly sacrifice was but a mite in comparison with the sacrifice sent from God. In keeping with the aforesaid principle that a sacrifice is not a sacrifice unless it costs the sacrificer something, God's Lamb cost Him much.

If Jehovah's anger was provoked toward Israel in the way they treated Moses insomuch that He threatened to wipe them out and make of Moses a great nation, then how much more was the heart of God moved when Jesus came unto His own and they received Him not! As the people mocked Christ they were mocking God, "He that hateth me hateth my

Father also" (John 15:23).

Precious Blood

"Forasmuch as ye know that ye were not redeemed with corruptible things, as silver and gold, from your vain conversation received by tradition from your fathers; but with the precious blood of Christ, as of a lamb without blemish and without spot" (1 Pet. 1:18-19).

The blood of Christ is precious. He is endeared to us by His blood and we to Him by the same. One meaning of the word "precious" is dear, as is often said, "They are precious people," etc. More accurately, precious means costly, valuable, honored or esteemed, and beloved. The precious blood therefore means the costly blood, valuable blood, honored blood, and beloved blood.

In 1 Peter 1:18 Peter tells us we are not redeemed with corruptible things, and in verse 19 he tells us we are redeemed by the blood of Christ. If we are not redeemed with corruptible things and we ARE redeemed by the blood, then the blood is *incorruptible*. In verse 18 the apostle informs that we are not redeemed with silver and gold. These two metals are among the most rare, valuable, and costly metals throughout the world. They are precious metals as compared with common metals like iron and lead. The blood of Christ is just as rare, valuable, and precious compared to common blood as are silver and gold compared to iron and lead. His blood is costly—the best God had to offer. It cost the Father and the Son much to provide salvation for us. His blood is rare—there is no other blood like it.

Paul admonished the Ephesian elders, " . . . feed the church of God, which he hath purchased with his own blood" (Acts 20:28). Notice that the name of Jesus is not mentioned in this verse at all. The second person of the Godhead has no direct reference by name. "He" and "His" are personal pronouns which refer back to the proper noun "God." It is true that "God is a Spirit," and that "flesh and blood cannot inherit the kingdom of God," however, God can make anything and everything. All the blood in Jesus' body was made by the creation power of the Father. For this reason Jesus' blood is of a higher type than common blood. We have a better covenant established upon better promises because better blood ratified it (see Hebrews 8:6).

Chapter Eight

RESTORATION BY THE BLOOD

Without contradiction Job is the oldest book in the Bible and what took place occurred long before the law was given. In this ancient book we see the blood message beautifully taught, although by a natural study apart from the Holy Spirit it would be impossible to grasp this message. There are many interpretations, and widely differing views concerning the book of Job. It is not our purpose to bring these forth or comment on the philosophical implications. Our study is concentrated on salvation and restoration by the blood, and from the first and last chapter of Job we will draw our discussion.

The Hedge

Job was a man who believed in and offered blood sacrifices. Satan would have smitten Job years before he did but was prevented by what the devil himself called a "hedge." Standing before God to give an account of his walks upon earth the adversary answered the Lord, "and said, Doth Job fear God for nought? Hast not Thou made an *hedge* about him, and about his house, and about all that he hath on every side? Thou hast blessed the work of his hands, and his substance is increased in the land" (Job 1:9-10).

The hedge of divine protection was in response to Job's burnt offerings which he offered continually (V. 5) and guarded five areas: Job, Job's house and family, Job's possessions, Job's works, and Job's substance.

Our blood protection today is a hedge that guards us on every side. Our *hedge protection* insures us of continued blessing from God. It is the author's opinion that today in the new covenant our protection is guaranteed in the blood of Christ and is not withdrawn from us at any time as we meet the conditions.

In this day of salvation only a believer can break his hedge. ". . . whoso breaketh an hedge, a serpent shall bite him" (Eccles. 10:8). The serpent cannot bite one who does not break his hedge. Today the adversary tempts us to disobedience that we might break our hedge. The believer who does not rule well over his own life is like a city broken down and without walls. He has no protection from satanic invasion (see Prov. 25:28).

Job: The Priest Of His Home

The Scriptures teach that a husband/father has the responsibility to provide for his family. This is true in the spiritual as well as the natural. The father sprinkled blood over his home in the behalf of his firstborn and family (see Exodus 12). The Philippian jailer was a husband and a father. Paul and Silas addressed this head of a home saying, "Believe on the

Lord Jesus Christ, and thou shalt be saved, AND THY HOUSE" (Acts 16:31). Job was acting on this principle long ago when he offered burnt sacrifices for his children:

> "And his sons went and feasted in their houses, every one his day; and sent and called for their three sisters to eat and to drink with them. And it was so, when the days of their feasting were gone about, that Job sent and sanctified them, and rose up early in the morning, and offered burnt offerings according to the number of them all: for Job said, It may be that my sons have sinned, and cursed God in their hearts. Thus Job did continually" (Job 1:4-5).

We have already seen how Cain and Abel did not offer sacrifice until they left home. In the same manner Job provided a blood covering for his sons and daughters all the while during his prosperity. There came a day when the hedge was removed and all his children and livestock were destroyed.

Twice As Much

We now leave Job chapter one and go to the end of the book. In chapter forty-two the Lord reproves Job's three friends for their wrong remarks. He instructs them, "Therefore take unto you now seven bullocks and seven rams, and go to my servant Job, and offer for yourselves a burnt offering; and my servant Job shall pray for you: for him will I accept" (Job 42:8). As the three friends offered the sacrifice, and the Lord accepted Job through the blood, the hedge was restored. The protection Job had known prior to the trial was once again in operation, but only after the sacrifices were offered. "And the LORD turned the captivity of Job, when he prayed for his friends: also the Lord gave Job *twice as much as he had before*" (V. 10). In chapter 1 verse 3 Job had 7,000 sheep, 3,000 camels, 500 yoke of oxen, and 500 she asses. In chapter 42 verse 12 where the Lord blessed the latter end of Job more than his beginning, he had twice the number of animals as he had before.

> "So the LORD blessed the latter end of
> Job more than his beginning: for he had
> fourteen thousand sheep, and six thousand
> camels, and a thousand yoke of oxen, and a
> thousand she asses" (42:12).

Everything Job had lost was restored to him double. We are restored in Christ "much more" than what we would have had only in Adam.

Salvation By The Blood

Not only had Job lost his cattle. He also lost his seven sons and three daughters. Chapter 1 verse 2, "And there were born unto him seven sons and three daughters." They died in a windstorm at the beginning of Job's calamities (see Job 1:18-19). At the end of the trial God promised to restore twice as much of everything Job lost. Following the same order Job would have fourteen sons and six daughters born to him (Chapter 42). Look at verse 13 and see how many sons and daughters he had following the turning of his captivity. "He had also seven sons and three daughters" (Job 42:13). Here is a beautiful truth. God did not give Job twice the number of sons and daughters because the first set of sons and daughters were atoned for by the blood. Job had not lost them

77

because they were saved! Job did actually have four-teen sons and six daughters. The first half were in Paradise and the second half were born to him in the restoration of "twice as much" of everything that he had. He did get double the number of cattle for when an animal dies it ceases to exist. The children who died in chapter one did not cease to exist. They were covered by Job's blood sacrifices and were accepted into Paradise. Therefore he got only the same number of sons and daughters (Chapter 42) because he had not really lost the first seven sons and three daughters. Meditate on this and you will see a beautiful type of salvation by the blood. ". . . the Lord gave Job twice as much as he had before."

Chapter Nine

THE OPEN FOUNTAIN

Jesus Christ is the focal object and central theme of the Word of God for He is the Word Himself (see Revelation 19:13). The One to whom the prophets spoke and of whom they prophesied is none other than our Lord. There has never been another individual who fulfilled biblical prophecy so perfectly and completely.

Zechariah foresaw a fountain flowing which provided cleansing for sin and for uncleanness:

"In that day there shall be a fountain opened to the house of David and to the inhabitants of Jerusalem for sin and for uncleanness" (Zech. 13:1).

Messianic prophecy refers often to a set day. Jesus referred to that day as His hour. At the onset of His ministry He stated, "Mine hour is not yet come" (John 2:4). Sometime later in ministering to His disciples He answered them saying, "The hour is come, that the Son of man should be glorified" (John 12:23). In contemplating about this hour he admitted, "Now is my soul troubled; and what shall I say?

79

Father, save me from this hour: But for this cause came I unto this hour. Father, glorify thy name. Then came there a voice from heaven saying, I have both glorified it, and will glorify it again" (John 12: 27-28). The day in which a fountain would be opened was the hour the Son of Man would be crucified. For the Lord of hosts had promised, "I will remove the iniquity of that land in one day" (Zech. 3:9). In a short day's time the Lamb of God took upon Himself the sin of the whole world.

We are living in that same day referred to by Paul as "the day of salvation . . . now is the acceptable time" (2 Cor. 6:2). The day Zechariah spoke of began when Jesus was nailed to the tree, and will continue right up to Armageddon. All the nations that come against Jerusalem will be divinely destroyed. The house of David and the inhabitants of Jerusalem will look upon their Deliverer from heaven whom they have previously pierced. They will ask, "What are these wounds in thine hands? Then he shall answer, Those with which I was wounded in the house of my friends" (Zech. 13:6; see also 12:9-14). They will realize the mistake their forefathers made many centuries ago and will accept Jesus as their Messiah. "And so all Israel shall be saved . . . " (Rom. 11:26).

Jesus Christ was a fountain sealed until the day His skin was pierced. When the skin of His body was broken the fountain was opened. Jesus is the Fountain. He is the source of the cleansing stream that washes away our sins. "Unto him that loved us, and washed us from our sins in his own blood" (Rev. 1:5).

God's Predetermined Plan

The Roman soldiers were not following their own plan of execution. They unknowingly followed a foreseen, foreknown, and fore-fixed plan devised before the world was even made. Peter caught a glimpse of the predetermined plan. In the first sermon preached in the day of salvation he stated, "Him, being *delivered by the determinate counsel* (predetermined plan) *and foreknowledge of God*, ye have taken, and by wicked hands have crucified and slain" (Acts 2:23). Jesus Christ was crucified according to a predetermined plan in the mind of God. This "determinate counsel" was the Godhead taking counsel of each other prior to the creation.

The Father foresees and foreknows. The exact manner in which Jesus would become the sin offering was laid out in eternity. In the revelation John also saw, ". . . the Lamb slain from the foundation of the world" (Rev. 13:8). The exact procedure to the very detail was foreknown. To this the prophets agree. It was foreseen in the Spirit that Christ would be spit upon and His beard plucked (see Isaiah 50:6). It was predetermined that His appearance would be marred (see Isaiah 52:14). It was foreknown that He would be smitten, pierced through, bruised, whipped, scourged, despised, oppressed, afflicted, and numbered with the criminals (see Isaiah 53). The Word pre-incarnate was spoken through David, "they have pierced my hands and my feet" (Ps. 22:16). Even in Deuteronomy the curse was put on those hung on a tree, foreshadowing the curse Jesus would bear (see Deuteronomy 22-23; Galatians 3:13). Jesus foretold His crucifixion saying, "And I, if I be lifted up from the earth, will draw all men unto me. This he said, signifying what (manner of) death he should die" (John 12:32-33).

In this light the Holy Spirit revealed the manner and procedure in which the Fountain was opened, and of its great importance to the child of God.

The order in which the five principle areas of His body were opened is of primary importance. We studied the three in-between areas (head, hands, feet) in Chapter 6, "Sanctification By The Blood," considering their spiritual importance. We will devote a full chapter to the spiritual importance of the fifth area being opened—His side—and will see why the water flowed. Likewise we will study the healing stripes in full detail. Now, however, we will focus our attention to the mechanical aspects of the crucifixion, or the physical aspects of Jesus' sacrifice: how the fountain was opened.

The BACK was opened with a Roman scourge outside Pilate's judgment hall at the whipping post. Jesus had been awake at least 24 hours at this time and was physically worn, as well as emotionally exhausted. The wonder that He survived the Roman scourge is remarkable. It goes to prove that no man could take His life from Him (see John 10:18).

The Roman scourge was far different from the commonly thought of cat-of-nine-tails which was developed centuries later. As all Roman weapons, it was precisionly built and masterfully employed. The sharp bronze metal tips pierced equally distant points into Jesus' back. The blows were placed high on the shoulder area and ripped the flesh in straight lines to the buttocks area. Christ foretold this experience in the Psalms describing His scourging as the plowing of a field. "The plowers plowed upon my back: they made long their furrows" (Ps. 129:3). The plowers were the Roman soldiers. They plowed with the

Roman scourge. They made long the stripes from the top to the bottom of His back. Again He speaks centuries before He was tied to the whipping post. "I gave My back to the smiters . . ." (Isa. 50:6). It is commonly thought that 39 blows were inflicted upon Him due to the custom of that time. The blood gushed from His back. Often historians record that victims of the scourge succumbed while tied at the post. The Father gave the Son strength to accomplish the predetermined plan. The mind of deity fore-planned the whipping post as the means by which the sicknesses and pains of many would be borne.

The crown of thorns woven from the common thornbush in the Mideast opened Jesus' HEAD to let the cleansing stream flow. Different from many thornbushes in North America, this bush had smaller thorns but many more of them. A sharply stinging poison resident in the thorn was released into His scalp as the mock crown was platted on His head and smitten with the reed (see Matthew 27:29-30). This stinging sensation caused a tormenting itching and burning. This pictures the poisonous thoughts the wicked have imagined. The blood flowed soaking this mock crown, showing the protection we have today from evil spirits. It is commonly known that the underpart or belly of a serpent is soft and that it cannot cross over sharp pointed objects. The desert birds, or roadrunners, assemble prickly cactus leaves surrounding a sleeping rattler. When it awakens from its afternoon siesta it finds itself imprisoned by the cactus needles. Unable to cross over the prickly barrier and fully frustrated the fangs are thrust into its own body and death shortly transpires. We have a protective hedge for our minds in the blood of Christ. The crown of thorns soaked with blood afforded the provision of "the helmet of salvation" (Eph. 6:17). If we keep our helmet on there can be no invasion of the enemy into our minds. Just as the smart Chapparal birds prepare a barrier for the snake, the Christian must make a sure defense for his thought life on the legal basis of the blood.

The last three areas of Jesus' body, our Fountain, were opened on the cross. HIS HANDS were nailed by the sharp Roman spikes into the wood. We have a certain idea that His hands were nailed directly over His head since the cross was a pole set upright. This would aid in causing the lungs to collapse more quickly than if they were nailed to a horizontal cross beam. The Greek word for hands includes the wrist area. It was probably through the middle of the wrists that the nails were driven. This would aid in holding the body since the nails would have torn through the palm area under the weight of His body.

HIS FEET were placed the one over the other while the spike was driven into His flesh. He was nailed while the timber pole was on the ground. Several soldiers heaved the pole with the sacrifice into the hole and it was dropped with a thud that jarred His body severely and caused the flesh to tear in His hands and feet. ". . . they pierced my hands and my feet" (Ps. 22:16).

It was the custom of the soldiers to break the legs of those still living toward late afternoon to speed up the death process. "But when they came to Jesus, and saw that he was dead already, they brake not his legs: But one of the soldiers with a spear pierced HIS SIDE, and forthwith came there out blood and water" (John 19:33-34). This fulfilled the

Scriptures once more for David said, "He keepeth all his bones: not one of them is broken" (Ps. 34:20).

Chapter Ten

WHERE IS THE NEW TESTAMENT?

The scene is the Last Supper in which Jesus eats the Passover with His disciples before His suffers. He has taken the bread and given it to them saying, "This is my body which is given for you: this do in remembrance of me." As He prepares to give them the cup He says, "This cup is the new testament in my blood, which is shed for you" (Luke 22:20). Mark the words: *"the new testament in my blood."* The new covenant is ratified, enacted, resident, and sealed in the blood of Jesus Christ. "This is the blood of the new testament . . ." (Mark 14:24). Without the blood there is no possible way He could have established a new covenant between God and man. The new testament (covenant, agreement, pact, promise, economy) is founded and based on the blood of Jesus.

The Blood Makes The Covenant

The old covenant between Jehovah and Israel was dedicated with blood. The transaction is recorded in the twenty-fourth chapter of Exodus. An insight into what really happened at that time is revealed in Hebrews 9:18-20:

"Whereupon neither the first testament was dedicated (inaugurated) without blood. For when Moses had spoken every precept to all the people according to the law, he took that blood of calves and of goats, with water, and scarlet wool, and hyssop, and sprinkled both the book, and all the people, saying, This is the blood of the testament which God hath enjoined unto you."

First, Moses sprinkled the book that contained the law of God. Sprinkling the blood upon the written record bound God to His word. Then, Moses sprinkled all the people with blood. This bound Israel to the covenant by the blood. An alternate rendering of verse twenty is, "This is the blood that makes the covenant by which God is joined to you." God was joined to Israel by the blood that made the covenant.

The written record of the new covenant is likewise sprinkled with blood. When a translator takes the blood out of the pages of the New Testament he is removing the seal of God from his translation. There are many new translations on the market today not worthy of the name. When the blood is taken out of the Scriptures the life of God is removed.

John writes, "And there are three that bear witness in earth, the (Holy) Spirit, and the water (of the Word), and the blood (of Christ): and these three agree in one" (1 John 5:8). The Spirit, the Word, and the blood give testimony concerning God and His program to men on earth. These three agree in one; they cannot be divorced from the other. Each has no function apart from the other two and must be seen as one unit. When one is removed the other two are removed as well. The churches that have removed the blood from their songs have taken the Spirit out of their worship. The Holy Spirit agrees with the blood of Christ. Theologians who have banished the blood from their teaching are no longer teaching God's word. The word and the blood agree.

The legal grounds for all of God's provisions rests upon the basis of the blood of Christ. The Word provides information on what these provisions are and instruction on how to enter into them. The Holy Spirit as the divine administrator over all of God's blessings ministers these provisions into our lives. One is not sufficient by itself. These three work together to give testimony to men.

The Blood Of Access

And then in similar comparison we, as Israel was, are likewise sprinkled with the blood. Just as the blood binds God to His people through His Word, the blood binds the people to God through His Word. The Spirit seals this operation. The Spirit bears witness to our spirit affirming that we are in the covenant. We are ushered before God's presence by the Holy Spirit according to the Word when sprinkled with Christ's blood. Peter describes this sprinkling. "Elect according to the foreknowledge of God the Father, through sanctification of the Spirit, unto obedience and sprinkling of the blood of Jesus Christ" (1 Pet. 1:2). Thus sprinkled, our basis of approach to God is guaranteed. "Having therefore, brethren, boldness to enter the holiest (Holy of Holies) *by the blood of Jesus*, by a new and living way, which he hath consecrated for us, through the veil, that is to say, his flesh . . ." (Heb. 10:19-20). The veil that separated the Holy of Holies from the Holy Place (in the earthly temple) was torn from top to bottom after Jesus bore our sins upon Calvary.

Immediately following the death of Jesus this 60-foot tall veil was rent in twain from top to bottom showing the rending had to be from above. If men had torn the veil it would have been torn from the bottom upwards. This was an act of God showing that the partition that separated man from a free access of approach to the Father was now gone. "And, behold, the veil of the temple was rent in twain from the top to the bottom" (Matt. 27:51).

A man can now approach God without human intermediary (priests, etc.) for Jesus has gone ahead as the forerunner and prepared the way. Jesus is now the High Priest and every believer is himself a priest. Unrestricted access to God and unhindered fellowship with Him is available to all who come by the blood of Jesus. This new and living way is the substance of what the old ceremonial way foreshadowed. In the old covenant only one man could go once a year where in the new convenant all may come daily. "Let us therefore come boldly unto the throne of grace, that we may obtain mercy, and find grace to help in time of need" (Heb. 4:16). We do not approach in fear of death as did the High Priest under the law. We come BOLDLY to obtain help from the throne.

A Better Covenant

If the first covenant had been faultless there would have been no need for a second (see Hebrews 8:7). "But now hath he obtained a much more excellent ministry, by how much also he is the mediator of a better covenant, which was established upon better promises" (Heb. 8:6). As a High Priest Jesus has a much more excellent ministry to God in our behalf for He does not offer the blood of bulls and goats which cannot take away sin (see Hebrews 10:4), but pleads our case to the Father by the merit of His own sacrifice. Our priest is our sacrifice. He intercedes for us His eternal blood and is thus able to save to the uttermost (see Hebrews 7:25).

The new covenant is better than the old for the blood that enacted it is better blood. The blood of bulls and goats could only sanctify ceremonially. The blood of Christ purges even the *conscience* of the believer (see Hebrews 9:13-14). Through the blood of the new covenant we have full access to God at all times. By His blood Jesus entered into the Holiest of all in Heaven and there intercedes in the place of full favor at the Father's right hand. "For Christ is not entered into the holy places made with hands (earthly tabernacle/temple built of stone), *which are figures of the true;* but INTO HEAVEN ITSELF, now to appear in the presence of God for us: Nor yet that he should offer himself often, as the high priest entereth into the holy place every year with blood of others . . ." (Heb. 9:24-25).

Jesus entered heaven itself there to appear before God FOR US not with the blood of others, but with His own blood. The earthly patterns (Mosaic temple) were of necessity purified with the blood of animals. But the heavenly things (mercy seat before the throne; corresponding to the mercy seat between the cherubim) were sanctified with better blood. Hebrews 9:22-23 tells us:

"And almost all things are by the law purged

with blood; and without shedding of blood is no remission. It was therefore necessary that the patterns of things in the heavens should be purified with these; but the heavenly things themselves with better sacrifices than these."

In Heaven our Great High Priest fulfilled the sprinkling of blood on the mercy seat in the same manner that the earthly high priest annually sprinkled the blood of one sin offering in the behalf of Israel. "Then shall he . . . bring his blood within the veil . . . and sprinkle it upon the mercy seat, and before the mercy seat: And he shall make an atonement . . . for all the congregation of Israel" (Lev. 16:15-17). When the blood was sprinkled seven times (V. 14) on the mercy seat and the ceremony completed the Day of Atonement resulted in a blood covering for a full year for the Israelites. The blood of bulls and goats accomplished an annual covering or atonement, while the blood of Christ has accomplished eternal redemption for the Church.

"But Christ being come an high priest of good things to come, by a greater and more perfect tabernacle, not made with hands, that is to say, not of this building; neither by the blood of goats and calves, but by his own blood he entered in once into the holy place, having obtained eternal redemption for us" (Heb. 9:11-12).

Jesus does not come before the Father once a year. He lives continually making intercession for the saints at the Father's right hand. We are saved from the guttermost to the uttermost when we come unto God by Him (see Hebrews 7:25). Jesus lives, "after

91

the power of an endless life" (Heb. 7:16). "Endless" means indestructible, inexhaustible, and unending.

Since Jesus has said that the new covenant is in His blood, every provision in this pact is based upon His blood. How true it is that every provision of God that we enjoy in this new and living way are automatically ratified by the blood of Christ. We will now consider how the four main provisions are directly related to the blood.

Forgiveness of sin is based directly on the blood of Jesus. "In whom we have redemption through his blood, the forgiveness of sins, according to the riches of his grace" (Eph. 1:7). "In whom we have redemption through his blood, even the forgiveness of sins" (Col. 1:14). "And without shedding of blood is no remission (forgiveness)" (Heb. 9:22).

Holiness of heart and life is based directly on the blood. "But if we walk in the light, as he is in the light, we have fellowship one with another, and the blood of Jesus Christ his Son cleanseth us from all sin" (1 John 1:7). "Wherefore Jesus also, that he might sanctify the people with his own blood, suffered without the gate" (Heb. 13:12).

Healing for the body was obtained by the blood that flowed from His back. "Surely he hath borne our sicknesses, and carried our pains" (Isa. 53:4). ". . . and with his stripes we are healed" (Isa. 53:5). Each of these statements has the double witness of a New Testament author. Matthew confirmed the message of Isaiah 53:4: "That it might be fulfilled which was spoken by Esaias (Isaiah) the prophet, saying, himself took our infirmities, and bare our sicknesses" (Matt. 8:17). Peter confirmed the message of Isaiah 53:5: ". . . by whose stripes ye were healed" (1 Peter 2:24).

Peter looks over his shoulder some 38 years or so and says, "were healed." Our healing is already an accomplished fact. To easily observe that we are healed by the blood of Christ one need only recognize the color of the healing stripes. As the red blood surfaced on the skin the stripes became visible.

The baptism with the Holy Spirit is pictured in the supernatural sign of the flowing water out of the crucified Christ's side. It was more than the clear fluid that collects in the chest cavity (which is not more than a few tablespoons). This was an actual stream of water that fulfilled the type of the water from the rock in the Old Testament and symbolized the living water Jesus gives to quench our thirst. "But one of the soldiers with a spear pierced his side, and forthwith came there out blood and water" (John 19: 34). We will fully develop this in a later chapter entitled, "That Rock Was Christ."

The Name Of Jesus

It is through the name of Jesus that the believer excercises his authority over demons and sickness (see Mark 16:15-18). It is in Jesus' name that we present our needs to the Father (see John 14:13-14; 16:23-24). If Jesus had not accomplished the will of God and had not established this new covenant in His blood, His name would have no power. There are two Scriptures which infer that the name has its authority on the basis of the blood.

"For where a testament is, there must also
of necessity be the death of the testator"
(Heb. 9:16).

Jesus is the testator of the New Testament. It was necessary that He die, and that He die shedding His blood. Had He not done this the new covenant would not have come into force. The name of the testator would not be effectual. The name of Jesus is effectual because of the death of the testator. The name of Jesus and its authority is a part of the overall covenant.

The second Scripture which reveals the authority of the name based on the blood in Luke 10:17-20:

> "And the seventy returned again with joy, saying, Lord even the devils (demons) are subject unto us *through thy name.* And he said unto them, I beheld Satan as lightning fall from heaven. Behold, I give unto you power to tread on serpents and scorpions, and over all the power of the enemy: and nothing shall by any means hurt you. Notwithstanding *in this rejoice not,* that the spirits are subject unto you; but rather *rejoice, because your names are written in heaven.*"

The seventy were not to rejoice that the demons were subject unto them but that their names were written in heaven. That is why the demons were subject unto them in Jesus' name. The seven sons of Sceva attempted to use the name of Jesus against evil spirits but were most unsuccessful. These Jewish exorcists were not believers in our Lord Jesus. Their names were not written in heaven and the demons did not come out (see Acts 19:13-17). The name of Jesus is ineffectual if the user is not washed from his sins in the blood knowing his name is written in heaven. (The obvious exception is when a sinner prays in Jesus' name for salvation, see Romans 10:13).

Chapter Eleven

WHERE DID JESUS BEAR OUR SIN?

There are a number of fine preachers who accept and teach that Jesus bore our sin in His spirit. It is upheld that Jesus spiritually suffered three days and nights in the torment of Gehenna fire. This is amazing since nowhere does Christ say He is in torment during the three day period between the crucifixion and the resurrection. Concerning the sin offering He said hanging on the cross, "It is finished" (John 19:30). How could it be complete, however, if He yet had to go and suffer in the flame? One well-known minister said it was in the flames of hell that Jesus defeated the devil. The Bible teaches most emphatically, however, that Satan is not in hell yet. Our adversary is still roaming over the face of the earth. The main Scripture from which this doctrine is developed is taken from Peter's sermon on the Day of Pentecost where he is quoting from the Psalms. "Because thou wilt not leave my soul in hell, neither wilt thou suffer thine Holy One to see corruption" (Acts 2:27; see Psalm 16:8-11). We heartily concur this refers to the lapse of time between the cross and the empty tomb.

95

The word for hell in the above verse is *hades* (Greek) which is the Old Testament counterpart of *sheol* (Hebrew). At death all souls, righteous and unrighteous, went to *sheol/hades* the realm of departed spirits. This realm was divided into two distinct and totally different compartments. Our Lord taught that the place the unrighteous went and still go is Gehenna (Greek: *geena*). The rich man said, "I am tormented in this flame" (Luke 16:24). Jesus referred to *Gehenna* as "hell fire" (see Matthew 5:22, 29-30; 10:28; 18:9; 23:33; Mark 9:43-47; Luke 12:5; 16:23).

The second compartment of *sheol/hades* was referred to as Abraham's bosom, or Paradise. This was a place of comfort that all the righteous dead under the old covenant departed to. It was not heaven where the throne of God is and where all the saved go to now at death. Today the righteous immediately depart at death to be with Christ in heaven (see 2 Corinthians 5:8; Philippians 1:21-24; Hebrews 12:23, Revelation 6:9-11). The change occurred when Jesus ascended on high leading captivity captive. It was for this purpose that He descended into the lower parts of the earth and that by the Spirit proclaimed the Gospel to the imprisoned spirits of dead men (see Ephesians 4:8-10; 1 Peter 3:18-22; 4:5-6).

What was the nature of Abraham's bosom? It is evident that father Abraham was in charge, and that all there were comforted (see Luke 16:19-31). Recall that Christ said to the believing malefactor while dying, "Today shalt thou be with me in paradise" (Luke 23:43). It would not have been a comforting thought to the dying thief had Jesus said, "Today shalt thou burn with Me in Gehenna." What would have been the use of calling on Jesus if he would have had to go to hell (Gehenna) fire anyway? Jesus told exactly where He was going at death. There can be no mistake. Paradise was the section of hades (usually rendered "hell" in the Authorized Version) of comfort. There was a great gulf fixed between Gehenna and Paradise. Once one was in one of the two he could not go to the other. Jesus Himself stated the following words quoting Abraham:

> "And beside all this, between us (Paradise) and you (Gehenna) there is a great gulf fixed: so that they which would pass from hence to you cannot; neither can they pass to us, that would come from thence" (Luke 16:26).

Since Jesus went to Paradise it is evident that He could not have gone to Gehenna. ". . . they which would pass from (here) to you cannot . . ." In other words Jesus went to Hades but not to Gehenna. At that time Paradise was just as much a part of Hades as was Gehenna. Since Christ went to Paradise and proclaimed the Gospel of His salvation to the righteous dead and led them in a train captive to God to Heaven. He moved Paradise from the realm of sheol/ hades to the third heaven. Jesus descended to go to Paradise into the bowels of the earth. When He ascended He carried Paradise with Him to heaven where all the righteous dead now are.

Paul was "caught up into paradise" which he stated is the "third heaven" (see 2 Cor. 12:1-4). The glorified Christ following His ascension said, "To him that overcometh will I give to eat of the tree of life, which is in the midst of the paradise of God" (Rev. 2:7). Because of the transition of Paradise from Hades to Heaven, all who are saved go to Heaven and all who are lost go to Hell.

Today, anyone in Hell can only be in the part known as Gehenna which Jesus again and again referred to as hell fire. Abraham's bosom has moved to Heaven. When Christ died, however, it was not so. Everyone went to Hades—either to Paradise or Gehenna. At the end of the age, Gehenna will be enlarged to the Lake of Fire. "And death and hell (hades, which will only contain Gehenna) were cast into the lake of fire" (Rev. 20:14). This will occur after the "great white throne" judgment (Rev. 20: 11-13) which, of course, is yet future.

Rather than suffering torment during the three days between crucifixion and resurrection, the preincarnate Word spoke through David, and was repeated by Peter, only two verses before the "hell" verse which has been so widely misinterpreted. These two verses are in the same passage in both Psalm 16:8-11 and Acts 2:25-28 where Jesus said His soul would not be left in hades. ". . . I (Christ) foresaw the Lord (the Father) always before my face, for he is on my right hand, that I should not be moved: therefore did my heart rejoice, and my tongue was glad; moreover also my flesh shall rest in hope . . ." (Acts 2:25-26). Christ was not suffering untold agony but rather was rejoicing and glad. At death His suffering was completed. He was "justified in the (Holy) Spirit" (1 Tim. 3:16) in that the Holy Spirit bore witness to His sacrifice, raising Him from the dead. Paul expressed, "And declared to be the Son of God with power, according to the spirit of holiness, by the resurrection from the dead . . ." (Rom. 1:4).

If Jesus did not bear our sin in His spirit and suffer agony in hell fire, just where did He bear our sin?

There are at least three places where the Word of God tells us where Jesus bore our sin. We need never be in doubt:

"Who his own self bare our sins in his own *body* on the tree, that we, being dead to sins, should live unto righteousness . . . " (1 Pet. 2:24).

"But now in Christ Jesus ye who sometimes were afar off are made nigh by the blood of Christ . . . having abolished in his *flesh* the enmity . . . that he might reconcile both unto God in one *body* by the cross, having slain the enmity thereby: And came and preached peace to you which were afar off, and to them that were nigh" (Eph. 2:13, 15-17).

What Happens To Sin?

There are many defeated Christians who have never learned how to overcome the attacks of the accuser because they are ignorant as to what happens to sin after they have confessed and forsaken it. They have been taught what happens to them, how they are cleansed, but not taught what God does to our transgressions.

By studying what God does to the confessed sin act and seeing the dramatic change of sin when it is removed the enemy will be totally unable to torment a believer with his regrettable past. It is God's desire that none of His children live under condemnation (see Romans 8:1).

The confessed sin is *blotted out* so that it is no longer visible in the sight of God. "I, even I, am he that blotteth out thy transgressions for mine own sake, and will not remember thy sins" (Isa. 43:25). Jesus accomplished this on the tree, "Blotting out the handwriting of ordinances that was against us, which was contrary to us, and took it out of the way, nailing it to his cross" (Col. 2:14). This blotting out of sins is pictured as a fog separating between the believer and his past: "I have blotted out, as a thick cloud, thy transgressions, and, as a cloud, thy sins: return unto me; for I have redeemed thee" (Isa. 44:22). A thick cloud on ground level is known as a fog. Occasionally we hear, "The fog was so thick it blanketed the city." This thick cloud has blanketed our forgiven past. Yet how often the Christian tries desperately to gaze into his past.

It is important to remember that God will not remember the sins He has forgiven. When God forgives He also forgets. "And their sins and iniquities will I remember no more" (Heb. 10:17). God has *forgotten* our sins promising, "I will not remember your sins." The Word does not say that God *can not* recall them. He said He *will not* recall them. He has drawn a curtain behind which all our sins are forgotten never to be remembered against us again.

Just because God has forgotten our sins does not mean Satan has. He still remembers our yielding to his temptations and attempts to place regret and guilt in us by causing us to remember them. What do we care if the devil remembers, anyway? We want to please God. Our Advocate stills the adversary's voice at this very hour before the throne of God.

Another Bible picture of the doing away of sin is seen in the Psalms. David was instructing his soul to bless the Lord for all His benefits. "Bless the LORD, O my soul . . . Who forgiveth all thine iniquities . . ." (Ps. 103:1,3). The Lord forgives all the iniquities of the soul.

Later in the Psalm David mused, "He hath not

dealt with us after our sins; nor rewarded us according to our iniquities. For as the heaven is high above the earth, so great is his mercy toward them that fear him. As far as the east is from the west, so far hath he *removed* our transgressions from us" (Psalm 103: 10-12). David did not know what science has learned in fairly recent generations. The Holy Spirit who inspired him knew full well for the Spirit had moved upon the face of the earth (Gen. 1:2). That is, that east and west never met but north and south do! If one goes north far enough he will be heading south after crossing the North Pole. Likewise, if one goes south far enough he will be travelling north after crossing the South Pole. You could travel east forever around this planet and never be heading west and vice-versa. David did not know this. This verse once more proves the inerrancy of the Scriptures. Had David said, "As far as the north is from the south, so far hath He removed our transgressions from us," he would be saying that we would eventually meet our sins again. However, since they are removed as far as the east is from the west we will never meet with them again. This is actually an immeasurable distance. God *removes* our sins from us.

A third illustration is found in Micah. "Who is a God like unto thee, that pardoneth iniquity, and passeth by the transgression of the remnant of his heritage? he retaineth not his anger forever, because he delighteth in mercy. He will turn again, he will have compassion upon us; he will subdue our iniquities; and thou will *cast* all their sins into the depth of the sea" (Mic. 7:18-19). Our sins are PLUNGED to the depths of the sea.

Within this century the depth of the sea has

101

been changed time after time. People used to accept three miles as the limit. Later it was changed to five miles deep. During the past few decades scientists have changed the record twice saying the ocean is seven miles deep, and later over eight miles deep. Only a few hundred feet under the surface and the ocean becomes very dark. Think how impossible it is that the naked eye could view something on the ocean's bottom. It takes specially-built equipment to explore the ocean's depths. Micah shows how far God has removed our sins. In his day it was impossible for anyone to submerge more than the diving depth of the sea. Our sins are plunged far below our remembrance of them, if we will accept it by faith.

King Hezekiah was extolling the Lord for His goodness. He had recovered from his terminal sickness and was praising God for the deliverance from death and extension of life. Remembering the sorrow his sickness had brought him he says, "Behold, for peace I had great bitterness: but thou hast in love to my soul delivered it from the pit of corruption: for *thou hast cast all my sins behind thy back*" (Isa. 38:17). God has cast all our sins behind His back. With the same arm that flung out the planets, God has hurled our sins backward, and they are still travelling at the speed of light away from God. Now why is it so important that God has cast our sins behind His back? "God is not a man that he should lie; neither the son of man that he should repent . . ." (Num. 23:19). The word "repent" means to turn around. God does not turn around. Because He has cast all our sins behind His back He will never look upon them ever again!

Chapter Twelve

THAT ROCK WAS CHRIST

Only a few days into the wilderness and the people of God found no water to drink. Rather than relying on the God who caused the waters to part to supply water, they murmured against Moses. Here we see the longsuffering and forbearance of God. If He marked our sins, who could stand before Him? After seeking the Lord Moses took the same rod he smote the sea with and smote the side of a large rock in Horeb. Rivers of water flowed from the inner recesses of this stone providing water for at least two million Israelites. "He opened the rock, and the waters gushed out; they ran in the dry places like a river" (Ps. 105:41). "He split the rocks in the wilderness, and gave them abundant drink like the ocean depths. He brought forth streams also from the rock, and caused waters to run down like rivers" (Ps. 78:15-16 NAS). There was an abundant supply of water for the thirsty multitudes in the barren wilderness desert.

Let's examine carefully the key verse:

"Behold, I will stand before thee there upon the rock in Horeb; and thou shalt smite the rock, and *there shall come water out of it*, that the people may drink. And Moses did so in the sight of the elders of Israel" (Exod. 17:6).

The Lord stood upon the rock picturing that it was He who would perform the supernatural in the behalf of His people. The reason God instructed Moses to smite the rock was that Christ, our Rock, would be smitten also. "There shall come water out of it," is rendered by many authorities as, "Out of its belly shall flow rivers of water." Jesus referred to this verse when He stated, ". . . as the scriptures hath said, out of his belly shall flow rivers of living water" (John 7:38). Apparently the only Scripture reference Jesus had in mind was in connection with this particular rock which brought forth streams. As Moses fulfilled this divine command before the elders of Israel, thousands of gallons of water poured out. There was and is no natural explanation for this tremendous outpouring. It was a supernatural act of Almighty God.

Paul comments on this wilderness experience in First Corinthians. He refers to Israel's passing through the sea, the covering of the cloud, the quail that flew in, and says in reference to the rock in Horeb: "And did all drink the same spiritual drink: for they drank of that spiritual Rock that followed them: and *that Rock was Christ*" (1 Cor. 10:4).

That which occurred to the rock in the wilderness also happened to the Rock on the cross. Moses took a rod and smote the side of the rock and water poured out of its side. Notice the parallel with the Rock on the cross, "But one of the soldiers with a spear pierced his side, and forthwith came out blood *and water"* (John 19:34). Likewise Christ was already dead (v. 30) when He was struck with a spear, and the wilderness rock was, of course, non-living matter. The water that poured from Christ's side was as supernaturally created as was the water from Horeb's rock. It was not clear fluid that collects in the chest; it was a sign from God. The desert rock provided water for physical thirst. The crucified Rock provided living water for spiritual thirst. Study the columnar illustration below to compare the similarities:

THE ROCK IN THE WILDERNESS	THE ROCK ON THE CROSS
was non-living,	was dead,
was struck with a rod,	was struck with a spear,
in the sight of Israel,	in the sight of Israel,
by one man, (Moses)	by one man, (soldier)
causing supernaturally created water to flow from its side,	causing supernaturally created water to flow from His side,
provided natural water for murmuring Israel.	providing the living water of the Holy Spirit for praising believers.

Speak To The Rock

Almost 38 years of wandering in the wilderness had passed by. Once more Israel found no water, and the children of the murmuring parents now quarreled with Moses because they had no water. This time, however, Moses allows resentment to enter his heart and eventually fails God, as indicated in Numbers 20:7-12:

"And the LORD spake unto Moses saying,

Take the rod, and gather thou the assembly together, thou, and Aaron thy brother, and *speak ye unto the rock* before their eyes; and it shall give forth his water, and thou shalt bring forth to them water out of the rock: so thou shalt give the congregation and their beasts drink. And Moses took the rod from before the LORD, as he commanded him. And Moses and Aaron gathered the congregation together before the rock, and he said unto them, Hear now, ye rebels; must we fetch you water out of this rock? And Moses lifted up his hand, and with his rod he smote the rock twice: and the water came out abundantly, and the congregation drank, and their beasts also. And the LORD spake unto Moses and Aaron, Because ye believed me not, to sanctify me in the eyes of the children of Israel, therefore ye shall not bring this congregation into the land which I have given them."

Angry toward Israel, Moses disobeyed God's instructions when he (1) implied that he and Aaron had to provide water, (2) addressed Israel instead of speaking to the rock, (3) smote the rock twice whereas he was to have taken his rod, the symbol of authority, and to hold it in his hand only.

To *speak* to this rock was all God commanded Moses to do. This would have shown Israel that the rock having been previously smitten, now needed only to be addressed. Speaking to the rock in faith would have caused water to flow as it had some years previously when smitten.

This rock typifies our Lord Jesus Christ and to

smite the rock the second time is the same as crucifying the Son of God afresh. Jesus was smitten once never to be smitten again. To crucify Christ again would mean His first offering was not enough. However, His first offering was His last for it was perfect. "But this man, after he had offered one sacrifice for sins for ever, sat down on the right hand of God" (Heb. 10:12). "So Christ was once offered to bear the sins of many . . ." (Heb. 9:28).

Jesus was crucified once at which time water poured from His belly. He now sits at the right hand of God and the Holy Spirit proceeds from the throne to the earth as believers speak to the Rock with praise and adoration. To get a drink from Jesus one needs not to crucify Him the second time but needs only to worship Him. As we ask in faith we receive. "Open thy mouth wide, and I will fill it" (Ps. 81:10).

Canaan is a type of the kingdom of God. Moses was not permitted to enter the land of promise because he smote the rock twice. This is symbolic that one who holds the Son of God to an open shame will be forbidden entrance into the kingdom of God (see Heb. 6:4-9). Moses' punishment was only figurative of this fact. He was not actually cut off from God, still the punishment was a most tragic one, for Moses had spent most of his life preparing for a land that was closed to him. Moses' disobedience was probably the most regrettable act of his entire life. We can learn the importance of obeying God from this event.

Drinking Of The Spirit

The same Gospel writer who recorded the flowing water from Christ's side also recorded the words of Christ depicting this event. Jesus taught that the

Holy Spirit would flow from Him to all who thirst, as told in John 7:37-39:

> "In the last day, that great day of the feast, Jesus stood and cried, saying, If any man thirst, let him come unto me, and drink. He that believeth on me, as the scripture hath said, out of his belly shall flow rivers of living water. (But this spake he of the Spirit, which they that believe on him should receive: for the Holy Ghost was not yet given; because that Jesus was not yet glorified.)"

As water was being poured out of earthen vessels on the last great day of the feast, Jesus stood and loudly said, "If any man thirst, let him come unto me, and drink." Here are three necessary requirements. (1) A man, any man, must sense and become acutely aware of his need for spiritual water. This desire must be as real to him spiritually as thirst is physically. The reason many do not drink is they have no real sincere desire for the Spirit. (2) A man must come to Jesus as the source of all spiritual blessings. Only through Jesus can one drink of the Spirit which proceeds from the Father. (3) The believer must drink. None drinks with his mouth closed, and this is likewise true in the spiritual realm. This involves asking. Jesus said, ". . . how much more shall your heavenly Father give the Holy Spirit to them that ask him?" (Luke 11:13). One must open his mouth wide believing God to fill it (see Ps. 81:10). We drink of the supernatural Spirit flowing from the supernatural Saviour with a supernatural utterance. It is here that the value of tongues comes into focus. The believer is "made to drink into one Spirit" by speaking in other tongues (see 1 Corinthians 12:13).

John 7:38 shows the ministry of the believer after his thirst has been quenched by drinking to the full of the living water: "He that believeth on me, as the scripture hath said, out of his belly (the believer's spirit) shall flow rivers of living water." It is important to note that although the believer has a release of the Spirit from within, Christ Himself is the only individual who actually had water flowing out of His belly just as the wilderness rock did. Some commentators read verse 38 this way: "He that believes on Me (*may drink from Me*), as the scripture hath said, Out of His belly (the Rock's) shall flow rivers of living water." They take it to mean that *his belly* is Christ's, not the believer's. We can accept this view as a believer has nothing to flow from his spirit while in a thirsty state and that only by drinking from that which flows from Christ is the believer able to in turn minister the same to others. The belly corresponds to the believer's spirit. Out of the regenerated, refreshed human spirit flows the Holy Spirit. This is outflow. Outflow is determined from inflow which is the Holy Spirit's flow into the believer's spirit, "proceeding out of the throne of God and of the Lamb" (Rev. 22:1).

A believer's rate of inflow is determined by the frequency and amount of the Spirit he drinks from the Rock as he speaks loving words of praise to Christ. Thus we can observe that the believer's ministry to others is dependent upon his fellowship with Christ. "A man can receive nothing, except it be given him from heaven" (John 3:27). We can minister nothing except that which we have received. Drinking is determined by speaking as can be seen in the Lord's instruction to Moses, "speak ye unto the rock"

(Num. 20:8). We are to "be being filled" with the Spirit speaking to ourselves in psalms, hymns, and spritual songs (see Ephesians 5:18-19). Realizing that Jesus has been smitten once forevermore to reign as King of kings and Lord of lords we can speak to the glorified Christ at the Father's right hand and drink to the full abundantly.

That there can be no doubt this living water is the Holy Spirit is seen in John's note of explanation given in parentheses in verse 39. "(But this spake he of the Spirit, which they that believe on him should receive: for the Holy Ghost was not yet given; because that Jesus was not yet glorified.)"

Believers should receive the Holy Spirit for believing involves receiving. "Have ye received the Holy Ghost since ye believed?" (Acts 19:2). Jesus has been glorified and the Holy Ghost has been given. Are you drinking daily of the Spirit? ". . . the Holy Ghost came on them; and they spake with tongues . . .' (Acts 19:6). If we truly believe Christ we will want all that He has for us.

Notice John's statement in 19:34: ". . . forthwith came there out blood and water." Some believe the blood flowed with the water in two separate but simultaneously flowing streams. Others believe that the blood flowed first and then water began flowing I prefer the second school of thought for one must first be cleansed by the blood of Jesus before he can receive the baptism with the Holy Spirit. Jesus said "Even the Spirit of truth *whom the world cannot receive* . . ." (John 14:17). The smitten rock and the death of Christ both resulted in outpourings of water The water Israel drank refreshed them so that they were able to win a battle with Amalek shortly after ward (see Exodus 17:8). The living water (the Holy Spirit) strengthens and refreshes the believer, making him victorious over the enemy.

Paul adds that the wilderness Rock followed Israel. That the literal boulder rolled alongside the Israelites is not the intended meaning. The "spiritual Rock" who was Christ, as the angel of the Lord followed or led Israel, throughout their wilderness experience. It was this angel whom Moses spoke to face to face.

Jesus accompanies the sojourning believer in all the earthly pilgrimage as a strong rock of defense and spiritual refreshing. "Lo, I am with you alway, even unto the end of the world" (Matt. 28:20). ". . . for he hath said, I will never leave thee, nor forsake thee. So that we may boldly say, The Lord is my helper, and I will not fear what man shall do (say and think) unto me" (Heb. 13:5-6).

He is always with us, and as our Rock we may speak unto Him in all situations of life, no matter what crises arrive, and drink freely of the water of life that He only can give.

When a Christian rejects the fullness of the Spirit he is telling Jesus, "Not all that you accomplished in my behalf do I accept or appreciate." Let's accept everything Jesus has provided for us.

Chapter Thirteen

A COMPARISON AND STUDY

Jesus was cursed on the tree in our place and bore our sin in His own body (see 1 Peter 2:24) He did not bear our sin in His blood. It was just as holy on the cross as it ever was. As He offered the sin sacrifice to God He was covered with pure, innocent, justifying, redeeming, sanctifying blood so that He was able to dismiss His spirit to the Father at death. He was drenched in His blood just as the living bird was dipped in the blood of the dead bird (Leviticus 14). For this reason His body was raised the third day and saw no corruption whatever.

The blood of Jesus is often preceded by a descriptive adjective in the Scriptures or a verse in which an adjective could be used to describe the nature and work of His blood. The adjectives given below do not always appear in that form in the verse but for our study they may be employed. We have limited our comments on these verses and would recommend that the student confess the blood with the adjective preceding it to realize what kind of blood Jesus shed for us. Example: "the justifying

112

blood"

Justifying

"Much more then, being now *justified by his blood*, we shall be saved from wrath through him" (Rom. 5:9).

Redeeming

"And they sung a new song, saying, Thou art worthy to take the book, and to open the seals thereof: for thou wast slain, and hast *redeemed us to God by thy blood* out of every kindred, and tongue, and people, and nation" (Rev. 5:9).

"In whom we have *redemption through his blood* . . . " (Eph. 1:7; Col. 1:14).

Remitting

"And almost all things are by the law purged with blood; and *without shedding of blood is no remission*" (Heb. 9:22).

Forgiving

"In whom we have redemption through his blood, *the forgiveness of sins*, according to the riches of his grace . . . " (Eph. 1:7)

"In whom we have redemption through His blood, even *the forgiveness of sins* . . . " (Col. 1:14).

Washing and Freeing

"And from Jesus Christ, who is the faithful witness, and the first begotten of the dead, and the prince of the kings of the earth. Unto Him that loved us and *washed us from our sins in his own blood*" (Rev. 1:5). Washed is also translated *"freed."* When a garment is soiled the dirt is freed from it as it is washed.

Purging

"How much more shall the blood of Christ, who through the eternal Spirit offered himself without spot to God, *purge your conscience* from dead works to serve the living God?" (Heb. 9:14).

Cleansing

"But if we walk in the light, as he is in the light, we have fellowship one with another, and the blood of Jesus Christ his Son *cleanseth us from all sin*" (1 John 1:7).

Sanctifying

"Wherefore Jesus also, that he might *sanctify the people with his own blood*, suffered without the gate" (Heb. 13:12).

Reconciling

"But now in Christ Jesus ye who sometimes were far off are *made nigh by the blood of Christ*" (Eph. 2:13).

Blotting

"*Blotting out the handwriting of ordinances that was against us*, which was contrary to us, and took it out of the way, nailing it to his cross . . . " (Col. 2:14).

Triumphing

"And having spoiled principalities and powers, he made a shew of them openly, *triumphing over them in it"* (Col. 2:15). "Spoiled" can be translated "divested Himself of" or "disarmed." This means Christ divested Satan of his authority. He completely disarmed all of Satan's hosts. Satan is a snake with a crushed head. Jesus fulfilled the first prophecy concerning the Messiah that was spoken directly to the serpent. "And I will put enmity between thee and the woman, and between thy seed and her seed; it shall bruise thy head, and thou shalt bruise his heel" (Gen. 3:15). Satan bruised Christ's heel with the sting of death at the cross. Jesus *crushed* the snake's head (literal meaning of bruise) on the resurrection morning. Jesus disarmed the enemy of all his power so that He could say prior to the Ascension, "All power is given unto me in heaven and in earth" (Matt. 28:18).

As God's policeman, our Lord took the gun of hell and death (or keys, see Revelation 1:18) out of the crook's hand. Since the Resurrection, "the devil ain't what he used to be," as some preachers put it. "For this purpose the Son of God was manifested, that he might destroy the works of the devil" (1 John 3:8). Through His death Jesus rendered helpless him that had the power of death, that is, the devil (see Hebrews 2:14-15). The only power the snake with a crushed head has today is the power of deception (see John 8:44). When a believer refuses to accept his lies, the enemy has no hold on him.

Overcoming and The Lamb
"And they *overcame him by the blood of the Lamb*, and by the word of their testimony; and they loved not their lives unto the death" (Rev. 12:11).

115

Agreeing

"And there are three that bear witness in earth, the Spirit, and the water, and the blood: and *these three agree in one*" (1 John 5:8).

Communing

"The cup of blessing which we bless, is it not *the communion of the blood* of Christ? The bread which we break, is it not the communion of the body of Christ?" (1 Cor. 10:16). The body of Christ must base its fellowship among the members upon the basis of the blood of Christ. The blood provides the basis of fellowship with other believers (see 1 John 1:7). The church is full of "seditions"—a work of the flesh for ignoring the communion of the blood (see Galatians 5:20).

Purchasing

" . . . feed the church of God, which he hath *purchased with his own blood*" (Acts 20:28).

Sprinkling

"And to Jesus the mediator of the new covenant, and to *the blood of sprinkling*, that speaketh better things than that of Abel" (Heb. 12:24).

"Elect according to the foreknowledge of God the Father, through sanctification of the Spirit, unto obedience and *sprinkling of the blood* of Jesus Christ . . . " (1 Pet. 1:2).

Speaking

" . . . that *speaketh better things* than that of Abel" (Heb. 12:24). If His blood is yet speaking, it is still living.

Incorruptible

"Forasmuch as ye know that ye were not redeemed with *corruptible* things, as silver and gold, from your vain conversation received by tradition from your fathers" (1 Pet. 1:18). Since we are not redeemed with corruptible things and are redeemed by the blood, it is incorruptible blood today.

Precious

"But with *the precious blood* of Christ, as of a lamb without blemish and without spot . . . " (1 Pet. 1:19).

Holy

"Of how much sorer punishment, suppose ye, shall he be thought worthy, who hath trodden under foot the Son of God, and *hath counted the blood* of the covenant, wherewith he was sanctified, *an unholy thing*, and hath done despite unto the Spirit of grace?" (Heb. 10:29). It is wrong to count the blood an unholy thing because it is holy blood.

Atoning

"For the life of the flesh is in the blood: and I have given it to you upon the altar to make an atonement for your souls: for it is *the blood* that *maketh an atonement* for the soul" (Lev. 17:11).

Innocent

"Saying, I have sinned in that I have betrayed *the innocent blood*" (Matt. 27:4).

Access

"Having therefore, brethren, boldness to enter

into *the holiest by the blood of Jesus"* (Heb. 10:19).

Perfect

"When Jesus therefore had received the vinegar, he said, *It is finished:* and he bowed his head, and gave up the ghost (spirit)" (John 19:30). "Finished" means perfect and complete. "It" refers to His blood sacrifice. His eyes saw the blood that drenched all about Him. His body, the cross, and the ground were covered with the blood.

Sheltering

"For the LORD will pass through to smite the Egyptians; and *when he seeth the blood* upon the lintel, and on the two side posts, *the LORD will pass (as a guard) over the door, and will not suffer (permit) the destroyer to come in* unto your houses to smite you" (Exod. 12:23).

Shed

"Likewise also the cup after supper, saying, This cup is the new testament in *my blood*, which *is shed* for you" (Luke 22:20).

Saving

"As for thee also, by the blood of thy covenant I have sent forth thy prisoners out of the pit wherein is no water" (Zech. 9:11). Zechariah speaks to those living in the new covenant time period. We were prisoners of the devil and were headed for the pit which has no water. In God's eyes we were already condemned to the pit because we were members of the kingdom of darkness. When we were translated into the kingdom of His dear Son, we were positionally removed from the judgment unto the second death which is the lake of fire. This has occurred by the blood of our better covenant which Zechariah foresaw.

The Scriptures teach that a person is whatever the blood is when he is covered with it. Take each of these 29 adjectives and confess you are what they are. Example: "I am redeemed because the redeeming blood covers me. I am saved because the saving blood covers me. I am protected because the sheltering blood covers me." We were guilty but when "the innocent blood" covered us we were made innocent.

COLUMNAR COMPARISON

The writer of Hebrews tells us, "He is the mediator of a better covenant, which was established upon better promises" (Heb. 8:6). For a better understanding of the better qualities resident in the new covenant as compared to the old we have provided a columnar comparison between the mechanics and operations of the two covenants. We have shown twelve main points of difference between the old and new covenants and given the Scripture references that you may look up to establish these points.

OLD COVENANT	NEW COVENANT
1. Was ratified by the blood of bulls and goats (Exod. 24:8; Heb. 9:19-20)	1. Was ratified by the better blood of Jesus Christ (Luke 22:20)
2. Provided only an annual covering on the	2. Obtained an eternal redemption for us (Heb.

Day of Atonement. (Lev. 16:12-19)	9:12)
3. High Priest entered the Holiest once a year and remained there only a short time (Lev. 16:30, 34; Heb. 9:7, 25)	3. Christ entered the Holiest in Heaven and ministers there as High Priest continually (Heb. 10:12; 8:2; 7:24-25; 6:20)
4. High Priest entered the Holiest without boldness in fear of death (Lev. 16:2)	4. Jesus destroyed the devil who had the power of death and delivered those who through fear of death were all their lifetime subject to bondage (Heb. 2:14-15)
5. No other Israelite was permitted to enter the Holiest ever—not even other priests (Heb. 9:6-7)	5. All brethren should have boldness to enter the Holiest by the blood of Jesus, by a new and living way which He has consecrated for us through His flesh (Heb. 10:19-23)
6. Could not take away sins and cleansed only the outward (Heb. 10:4; 9:13)	6. Cleanses from all sin and purges the conscience of the worshipper (Heb. 9:14; 1 John 1:7, 9)

7. The veil separated from God's presence (Heb. 9:3-5)

7. The veil was supernaturally torn in half exposing the Holiest (Matt. 27:51; Heb. 6:19-20; 9:8)

8. God has made the first covenant old and ready to vanish away. He promised those living under this covenant that He would make a new one (Heb. 8:8-13)

8. God has accepted Christ's sacrifice and made this the everlasting covenant in which His promise to Abraham is fulfilled (Heb. 13:20; Gal. 3:29)

9. The law is good in that it provides shadows of the work of Christ but no longer provides a means of access to God (Heb. 10:1)

9. Christ is the end of the law for righteousness to everyone that believes (Rom. 10:4)

10. In the end never made anyone perfect (Gal. 3:11; Heb. 10:1-2)

10. The Great Shepherd through the blood of the everlasting covenant makes the Christian perfect in every good work to do His will (Heb. 13:21)

11. The High Priests died and were replaced (Heb. 7:23-25)

11. Jesus lives after the power of an endless, indestructible,

	inexhaustible, resurrection life (Heb. 7:16)
12. At death a righteous Israelite departed to Abraham's bosom known as Paradise in sheol/hades (Luke 16:22)	12. At death the believer departs to be in the presence of the Lord (with Christ) which is far better (2 Cor. 5:8; Phil. 1:21-23)

In the light of the above scriptural comparisons, is it any wonder that the writer of Hebrews calls the new covenant the better one?

* * * * *

Address all personal comments, prayer requests, counseling needs, and requests for ministry to:

David Alsobrook
Route 1, Box 31
West Paducah, Kentucky 42086

ABOUT THE AUTHOR

David Alsobrook was born and raised in a minister's home. He rebelled against the church's teachings at an early age and became involved in all forms of teenage sins. At the age of 15 David was genuinely born again and thirsted for the knowledge of God. This led to an intense hunger for the Word. He read the Bible through four times in the first six months of his Christian life. Since then he has devoted himself to the study and ministry of the Word of God. He has witnessed many miraculous confirmations to his ministry in healing and deliverance, and is ever travelling the country and abroad preaching and teaching the Kingdom of God on a wide variety of topics.

Dianne travels with her husband and assists in ministering to people's needs. Whenever they are not on the road they reside at home in West Paducah, Kentucky.

TAPES

Tapes are sent for a donation of only $1.50 each! (Please give exact number of copies you would like to have.)

Angels
Atmosphere of Praise
The Baptism From Job
The Baptism in the Holy
  Spirit
Beautiful Garments
The Blood Covenant
By My Spirit
Cain and Abel
Choruses
Christ Is All
Cleansing the Leper
Dancing Before the Lord
The Fountain Opened
The Fruit of the Spirit
The Gift of Prophecy
God's Great Army
The Happy Man
Heavenfire
Healing the Bruise
Holiness
Holiness Is the Key
Inner Healing
Introduction to Spiritual Gifts
Jeremiah's Call
Jesus Christ Is in You
Jesus the Carpenter
Joshua's Example
King "I" Died
Kings and Priests
Know Your Enemy
The Lamb and the Dove
Lamb Requirements
The Mind of Christ
Ministry Gifts of Christ
More on Holiness
Only God Can Make a Tree
Praise
Renewing Your Mind
Seven Steps to Restoration
The Seven Temples

Shake It Off
The Song of the Lord
Spiritual Songs
The Spirit Without Measure
Staying Free
Symptoms of Demonic
  Behavior
True Worship
The Value of Tongues
A Vessel Unto Honor
Waters to Swim In/I Love My
  Master
The Way of Peace
Ways to Praise God
What Are Demons Like?
Wrong Concepts Corrected